BASICS IN PRONUNCIATION

INTERMEDIATE PRACTICE FOR CLEAR COMMUNICATION

LINDA LANE
American Language Program
Columbia University

Acknowledgments

I am indebted to a number of people whose support, suggestions, patience, and good humor made this book possible. I am grateful for the help and suggestions of my editors at Longman, Debbie Sistino, Christine Cervoni, and Janet Battiste; for the reminders and encouragement given to me by Wendie Saxton from Columbia University; for the suggestions and advice of my colleagues at the American Language Program, who used these materials in their own classes; and for the encouragement and patience of my family, Mile, Martha, Sonia, and Luke, and of my dear friend Mary.

Mostly, I want to thank my students—for teaching me how they learn pronunciation, for wanting to improve their pronunciation, and for showing me how to help them.

Basics in Pronunciation

Pearson Education, 10 Bank Street, White Plains, NY 10606

Editorial Director: Joanne Dresner
Senior Acquisitions Editor: Allen Ascher
Development Editor: Debbie Sistino
Production Editor: Christine Cervoni
Cover Design Adaptation: Joe DePinho
Text Design: Cavazos Art and Design, Inc.
Text Art: Lloyd Birmingham, pages 151, 154, Daisy de Puthod

Library of Congress Cataloging-in-Publication Data
Lane, Linda (Linda L.)
　　Basics in pronunciation / Linda Lane.
　　　　p.　　cm.
　　ISBN 0-201-87806-2
　　1. English language—Textbooks for foreign speakers.　2. English
language—Pronunciation.　　I. Title.
PE1128.L3376　1997
428.2'4—dc21　　　　　　　　　　　　　　96-50194
　　　　　　　　　　　　　　　　　　　　　　　CIP

8 9 10 11 12 13 14 15 CRS 070605040302

CONTENTS

INTRODUCTION

Basics in Pronunciation is a comprehensive course that helps intermediate students speak English more clearly and accurately. The course integrates all aspects of pronunciation—sounds, stress, rhythm, and intonation.

Each unit in *Basics in Pronunciation* is designed to make students aware of a particular pronunciation point or feature. Students first work on controlled activities that allow them to develop skill and proficiency with the particular point. They then practice the point in freer, communicative activities. The activities are designed to ensure student involvement and include playing games, working with information on high-interest topics, and learning idioms. Units end with homework assignments for students to tape-record.

The three classroom audiocassettes that accompany *Basics in Pronunciation* have all the recorded activities for the course. Recorded material is marked with ⌒ in the text. In addition, there is a self-study cassette that allows students to listen on their own. Material included on this audiocassette is marked with an *S* inside the headphone icon ⌒S⌐ .

Organization of the Book

Basics in Pronunciation has two main parts: "Getting an Overview" and "Basic Features in Pronunciation."

Part I, Getting an Overview: These six units present the phonetic symbols used in the book and provide overviews of English consonants, vowels, stress, rhythm, and intonation. They help students build an awareness of English pronunciation by providing them with opportunities to experiment with the sounds and patterns of English.

Part II, Basic Features in Pronunciation: This part is divided into three sections: (1) Vowels and Vowel Contrasts; (2) Consonants; and (3) Stress, Rhythm, and Intonation. Its thirty-four units provide practice with specific sounds in English and suprasegmentals such as word stress, thought groups, and rising and falling intonation.

Units in *Basics in Pronunciation* typically have the following setup:
- **Explanatory material:** This section, for presentation and reference, shows how sounds are articulated or presents useful material on the pronunciation feature.
- **Practice:** This section contains a variety of interactive activities. These typically include practicing sounds in words, listening activities, and opportunities for students to practice pronunciation in natural communication and dialogues.
- **Homework:** Students tape-record assignments onto their own cassettes and give them to the teacher for review and comments.

PART I

Getting an Overview

UNIT 1

THE PHONETIC ALPHABET

The phonetic alphabet shows the sounds of words. In this book, phonetic symbols will be used to show how a word is pronounced. You should become familiar with the phonetic symbols. Phonetic symbols will usually be placed in square brackets to show that they are different from the letters used in spelling. For example, the last sound of *nice* is [s]: [s] is the symbol of the last sound; the letters *ce* are the spelling of this sound.

Familiar Consonant Symbols

Many of the phonetic symbols for consonant sounds are the same as the letters commonly used to spell the sounds. Listen to the examples.

[b]	boat	[l]	late	[t]	two
[d]	down	[m]	man	[v]	very
[f]	fish	[n]	not	[w]	want
[g]	go	[p]	post	[y]	yes
[h]	home	[r]	red	[z]	zero, laser
[k]	kiss, cold	[s]	sick, nice		

Different Consonant Symbols

Some consonant sounds are written with special symbols. Listen to the examples.

[θ]	think	[θɪŋk]
[ð]	this	[ðɪs]
[ʃ]	ship	[ʃɪp]
[ʒ]	pleasure	[plɛʒər]
[tʃ]	check	[tʃɛk]
[dʒ]	judge	[dʒədʒ]
[ŋ]	sing	[sɪŋ]

🎧 Vowel Symbols

It is important to be familiar with the phonetic symbols for vowel sounds, since the same vowel sound may be spelled in different ways. Look at the symbols and listen to the examples.

[ɑ]	far, not	[fɑr, nɑt]
[ɛ]	get, bread	[gɛt, brɛd]
[ɔ]	bought, all	[bɔt, ɔl]
[ə]	but, other	[bət, əðər]
[æ]	sad	[sæd]
[ɪ]	kiss	[kɪs]
[ʊ]	book, put	[bʊk, pʊt]
[iy]	see, leaf	[siy, liyf]
[ey]	say, raise	[sey, reyz]
[ow]	no, boat	[now, bowt]
[uw]	rude, cool	[ruwd, kuwl]
[ay]	die, wine	[day, wayn]
[aw]	house, now	[haws, naw]
[oy]	boy, noise	[boy, noyz]

🎧 Stress Markings

Primary or heavy stress (´) and secondary stress (`) are marked above the syllable. Unstressed syllables will sometimes be marked with ˘. Listen to the examples.

tŏdáy   ráilròad

◢◤◢◤◢◤◢◤◢ Practice ◤◢◤◢◤◢◤◢◤

1. The words below are written phonetically. Look at the symbols above to help you figure out the word. Write the word with its regular spelling.

1. [haws] _____house_____

2. [ʃow] _____

3. [dʒæz] _____

4. [wɛ́ðər] _____

5. [rayt] _____

6. [bʊk] _____

7. [tuwθ] _____

8. [síŋɪŋ] _____

2. Listen to these words. Write the phonetic symbol for the bold-faced letters.

1. **sh**op _____ ʃ _____

5. **ch**eck _____

2. **th**anks _____

6. tou**gh** _____

3. ro**s**e _____

7. cau**ght** _____

4. **wr**ong _____

8. sho**pped** _____

Note: You may be familiar with some phonetic symbols which are different from the ones used in this book. Alternative symbols are shown below on the right side of the equation.

1. [y = j]
2. [ʃ = š]
3. [ʒ = ž]
4. [tʃ = tš, č]
5. [dʒ = dž, ǰ]

6. [ə́ = ʌ]
7. [ə́r = ɝ]
8. [ər (unstressed) = ɚ]
9. [iy = ii, i:]
10. [ey = ei]

11. [ow = ou]
12. [uw = uu, u:]
13. [ay = ai]
14. [aw = au]
15. [oy = ɔi, oi]

Related Unit ▶ 2

U N I T 2

L E T T E R   N A M E S   O F
T H E   R E G U L A R   A L P H A B E T

English words are spelled with the twenty-six letters of the "regular" alphabet. (The phonetic alphabet, which shows the sounds of English, has more than twenty-six phonetic symbols, because English has more than twenty-six sounds.) It is important to know the names of the letters of the regular alphabet in order to spell words. Try pronouncing the alphabet using the phonetic symbols next to each letter.

Listen to the names of the letters.

A	[ey]	N	[ɛn]
B	[biy]	O	[ow]
C	[siy]	P	[piy]
D	[diy]	Q	[kyuw]
E	[iy]	R	[ɑr]
F	[ɛf]	S	[ɛs]
G	[dʒiy]	T	[tiy]
H	[eytʃ]	U	[yuw]
I	[ay]	V	[viy]
J	[dʒey]	W	[dəbəl yuw] ("double u")
K	[key]	X	[ɛks]
L	[ɛl]	Y	[way]
M	[ɛm]	Z	[ziy]

Practice

1. Ask a classmate how to spell his or her first and last names.

   Example: A: _____Juan_____, *how do you spell your name?*

   B: *J - U - A - N   M - E - N - D - O - Z - A*

2. Sometimes the name of a letter sounds the same as a word in English. For example, the name of the letter *U* sounds the same as the pronoun *you*. Sometimes, when we take notes, we can abbreviate words using single letters. Look at the letters below and try to figure out the phrase or sentence. Then write the sentence as it is normally spelled. Can you think of others?

Example: I O U $5. _____I owe you $5._____

1. I C U _____

2. Y R U sad? _____

3. R U O K? _____

4. 4 U _____

Related Unit ▶ 1

UNIT 3

OVERVIEW OF THE VOWELS

There are fourteen vowel sounds in English: eleven vowels and three diphthongs (vowel + [w] or [y]). Different positions of the tongue result in different vowel sounds. Look at the chart of the vowels. The placement of the vowels shows their position in the mouth.

Some English vowels, like the vowels in *seen* and *sin*, occur in "tense-lax" pairs. The vowel in *seen* is a tense vowel and the vowel in *sin* is a lax (relaxed) vowel. The tongue position with lax vowels is closer to the center of the mouth than with tense vowels.

Look at the chart and listen to the vowels.

ENGLISH VOWELS

		Front	Central	Back
High	Tense	Pete [iy]		boot [uw]
	Lax	pit [ɪ]		put [ʊ]
Mid	Tense	bait [ey]	but [ə]	boat [ow]
	Lax	bet [ɛ]		
Low				bought [ɔ]
		bat [æ]		
			pot [ɑ]	

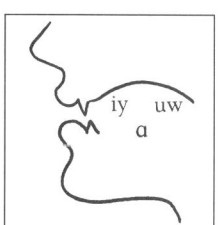

Diphthongs: my [ay]   how [aw]   boy [oy]

Follow the instructions.

1. Using a mirror, say *Pete-pot-Pete-pot-Pete-pot* slowly. Describe what is happening to the openness of your mouth as you change from *Pete* to *pot*. (If you do not have a mirror, watch another classmate.)

2. Say *see-Sue-see-Sue-see-Sue* very slowly. Concentrate on where your tongue is as you move from *see* to *Sue*. Now repeat the same two words. Using a mirror (or looking at a classmate), describe what happens to your lips as you change from *see* to *Sue*.

3. The four English vowels [iy, ey, uw, ow] (*Pete, bait, boot, boat)* are called "impure" vowels because they end in a short [y] or [w] sound. For [iy, ey] (*Pete, bait)*, the tongue slides up and front to make the [y] sound after the vowel. For [uw, ow], the lips continue rounding to make the [w] sound after the vowel. The [y] and [w] sounds after the vowels are important to pronouncing English correctly. They can be heard most easily when the next word starts with a vowel.

   In these phrases, a small *y* or *w* has been added when the spelling does not show the sound. The linking of [y] or [w] to the next vowel is shown with a curved underline. Listen and repeat the phrases. Try to hear the [y] or [w].

[iy]	[ey]	[uw]	[ow]
1. see^{y}us	3. say‿it	5. do^{w}it	7. go^{w}up
2. be^{y}over	4. pay‿Ann	6. too^{w}easy	8. show‿us

4. Listen and repeat the words. Write a small *y* or *w* to show the linking sound between the two bold-faced vowels.

1. p o^{w}e t	3. b e a b l e	5. g e o l o g y	7. g r a d u a l
2. g o o n	4. c r e a t i o n	6. v i d e o	8. q u i e t

Related Units ▶ 7, 8, 9, 10, 11, 12, 13, 14, 15, 16, 31, 35

UNIT 4

OVERVIEW OF THE CONSONANTS

There are twenty-four consonants in English. Many of them, like the first sound in *ten*, are similar to consonants in other languages. A few, however, like the first sound in *thing*, are less common and may be difficult to pronounce.

Most consonants are made by touching the tongue to some part of the mouth. The purpose of this unit is to help you become aware of what is inside your mouth and how different positions of the mouth produce different sounds. In later units, you will practice the consonants individually.

Inside Your Mouth: The Vocal Organs

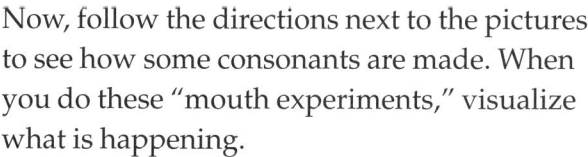

Look at the cross-section (side view) of the vocal organs used to produce English consonants. The vocal organs are described in the following sections. Use the tip of your tongue to touch your lips, your teeth, your alveolar ridge (the small, flat part behind the top teeth), and the palate. Try to picture these parts of your mouth as you touch them.

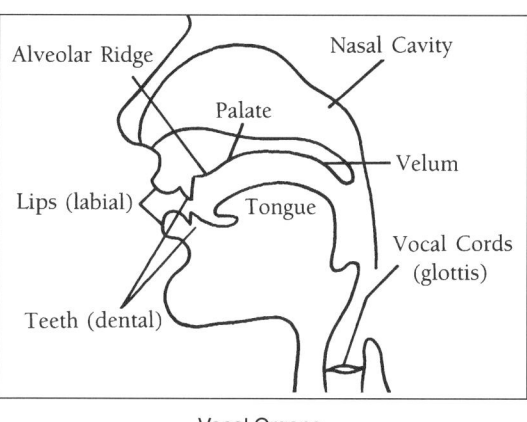

Vocal Organs

Now, follow the directions next to the pictures to see how some consonants are made. When you do these "mouth experiments," visualize what is happening.

Press your lips together and say *P*. Look at a classmate's lips when he or she says *P*. What other sounds are made with the lips?

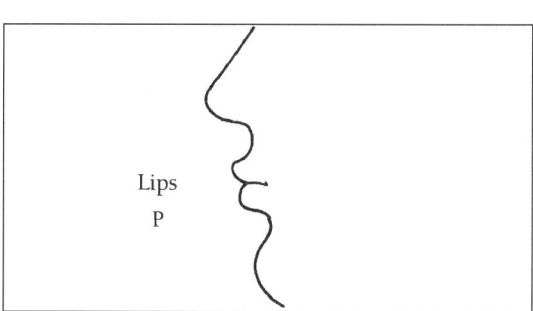

Place the tip of the tongue behind the top teeth and feel the small, flat part behind the teeth, the alveolar ridge. Put your mouth in position to say *T*, but don't say it. Hold the position and feel where the tongue is touching.

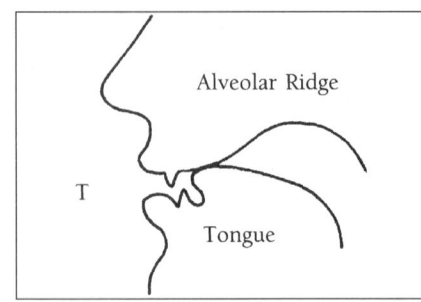

Voiced and Voiceless Sounds

Look at the cross-section of the vocal organs again and find the vocal cords or glottis. When the vocal cords vibrate, voiced sounds are produced. You can feel the vibration with your hand.

Make a long [zzzzz], placing your fingers against the front side of your throat, and feel the vibration. [z] is a voiced sound. Now make a long [sssssss], with your fingers in the same position. [s] is a voiceless sound. What do you feel? Now, keeping your fingers in the same position, switch back and forth between the two sounds: [zzzzsssszzzzssssszzzzssss]. Feel the vibration turn on and off.

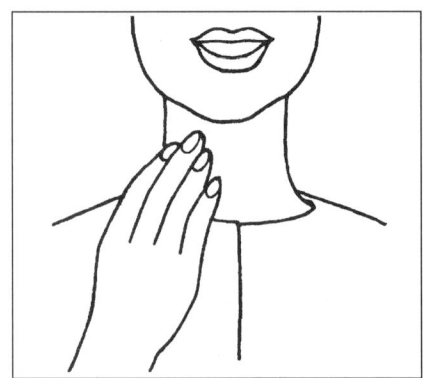

The Air Flow

In addition to knowing where a consonant is pronounced and whether the sound is voiced or voiceless, it is also useful to know what happens to the air flow. This section gives some examples of different types of sounds produced by changes in the air flow.

- **Stop consonants** are produced when the air flow is completely stopped for a moment. Put your mouth in position to say *pie*, but do not say it. Hold the position and try to breathe (through your mouth). For a brief moment, you will not able to breathe because [p] is a stop consonant. Are [d] and [t] stop consonants? Try the same experiment. Put your mouth in position to say *do* and *too*, but don't say them. Hold the position and try to breathe through your mouth. Can you do it?

- **Fricatives** are another group of consonant sounds. They are made by blocking the air but not completely stopping it. Fricatives have a "noisy" sound. You can breathe out through them, but not easily. Try breathing through some fricative sounds: [vvvvvvvvvvv], [sssssssssss], [ʃʃʃʃʃʃʃʃʃʃ].

- **Affricates** combine a stop and a fricative. There are two affricates in English: the last sound in *much* ([tʃ]) and in *age* ([dʒ]). With [tʃ] and [dʒ], you will not hear the stops [t] and [d] as separate sounds. You can hear that they are stops because they briefly "cut off" the preceding vowel sound. Say the word pairs below. The first word ends in an affricate, and the vowel is briefly stopped. The second word ends in a fricative, and the vowel is never completely stopped.

much [tʃ]   mush [ʃ]   legion [dʒ]   lesion [ʒ]

English Consonants

The chart below shows all of the consonants in English. The columns show where the consonant is pronounced in the mouth. The rows show whether the consonant is voiced (Vd) or voiceless (Vl) and what happens to the air flow.

ENGLISH CONSONANTS

		Labial	Labio-Dental	Interdental	Alveolar	Palatal	Velar	Glottal
Stop	**Vl**	p			t		k	
	Vd	b			d		g	
Fricatives	**Vl**		f	θ	s	ʃ		h
	Vd		v	ð	z	ʒ		
Affricate	**Vl**					tʃ		
	Vd					dʒ		
Nasal	**Vd**	m			n		ŋ	
Liquid	**Vd**				l, r			
Glide	**Vd**	w				y		

Beginning and Final Consonants

Beginning voiceless stop consonants in English are strongly pronounced with a puff of air called "aspiration" (written ʻ: *pʻie*). Final stop consonants and final voiced fricatives are pronounced, but not released strongly (written ʼ: *eatʼ*).

pʻill   lipʼ

tʻea   eatʼ

Kʻay   acheʼ [eyk]

Pronounce the sounds and answer the questions.

1. Hold your fingers against the front side of your throat and say some voiced fricatives. Feel the vibration.

   [vvvvvv]   [zzzzzz]   [ʒʒʒʒʒʒ]

   Keeping your fingers in the same position, say these voiceless fricatives.

   [ffffff]   [ssssss]   [ʃʃʃʃʃʃ]

2. Say the word *we* very slowly. What happens to the lips to make [w]? Check this by looking at a classmate's mouth as he or she says *we*. Do the same thing with the word *how* [haw]. What happens to the lips when a final [w] is made? What is the difference between a beginning and final [w]? (Hint: When do the lips start in a rounded position? When do they end in a rounded position?)

3. Pretend you have just run a mile and are breathing heavily. What English consonant sound are you making?

4. Say these words and repeat them very slowly.

   catch   **ca**sh

   What is the difference between the two vowels? What difference between the two final consonants causes the vowel difference?

Related Units ▶ 17, 18, 19, 20, 21, 22, 23, 24, 25, 26, 27, 28, 29, 30, 33

UNIT 5

SYLLABLES AND STRESS

Syllable

A syllable is a "beat" of a word. The word *visit* has two syllables or beats.

visit

In English, syllables usually contain a vowel and may also contain one or more consonants. In most words, a syllable break occurs between a vowel and a consonant: *v i / s i t*.

When there are two consonants inside a word, the syllable break usually occurs between the consonants: *f a s / t e r*. It is not important to know exactly where a syllable begins or ends, but it is very important to know how many syllables a word has.

Stress

In English words with two or more syllables, one of the syllables is stressed (written ´) and is pronounced longer and louder than the other syllables. In the word *visit,* the first syllable is stressed and is longer and louder than the second syllable.

vísit

Pitch and Stress

Syllables that have primary stress may also be pronounced on a higher pitch (musical note) than unstressed syllables. In one-syllable words and words stressed on the last syllable, pitch usually starts high and then drops gradually.

sád   ónce   arríve   deláy   vísit   háppen

"Dropped" Syllables

In some words, unstressed syllables are rarely pronounced, even though they are written. For example, the word *every* looks like a three-syllable word. However, most speakers "drop" the middle syllable and pronounce it as a two-syllable word.

é v ǿ r y

The spelling of *comfortable* makes it especially difficult to pronounce. Most people do not pronounce the second *o* and, in addition, pronounce the [t] before the [r].

c ó m f ǿ r t a b l e   [kə́m f tər bəl]

Vowel + Vowel Sequences

In some words, two vowel letters written together may represent only one vowel sound, as in *bread*, *piece*, *boat*, and *four*.

In other words, like *science,* the two vowel letters represent two vowel sounds, pronounced in separate syllables. Usually the first vowel sound ends in an unwritten [y] or [w] sound (for example, the vowels [iy], [ay], and [uw]). The unwritten [y] or [w] sound is used to join the two syllables.

s c i ͬʸe n c e   [sáyəns]

Practice

1. **Hearing Syllables.** Listen carefully to the words. In each word, there is a vowel letter that is not pronounced. Draw a line through the unpronounced vowel, underline the syllables, and write the number of syllables in the blank. Mark the stressed syllable with a ´. Then choose four words and say them out loud.

1. génǿral _2_   5. favorite ____   9. different ____   13. federal ____

2. business ____   6. opera ____   10. evening ____   14. practically ____

3. interest ____   7. vegetables ____   11. average ____   15. family ____

4. aspirin ____   8. interested ____   12. camera ____   16. temperature ____

2. Vowel + Vowel Sequences.

In these words, the two bold-faced letters are pronounced as separate vowel sounds in separate syllables. They are joined with an unwritten [y] or [w] sound. Listen carefully to the words. If you hear a [y] sound, write a small *y* between the vowels; if you hear a [w] sound, write a small *w* between the vowels. Underline the syllables and mark the stressed syllable. Then choose four words and say them out loud.

1. pi^yáno
2. gradu**a**te
3. appl**ia**nce
4. g**eo**graphy
5. c**oo**peration
6. pron**u**nc**ia**tion
7. sit**ua**tion
8. exper**ie**nce
9. p**oe**try

3. Hearing Syllables.

Listen carefully to the words. In the blank, write *1* if the two vowel letters are pronounced as a single vowel. Write *2* if they are pronounced as two vowels in separate syllables. If they are pronounced as two vowels, write the [y] or [w] sounds between the two vowels. Mark the stressed syllable. Then choose five words and say them out loud.

1. bre'ak __1__
2. cre^yáte __2__
3. n**eo**n ____
4. p**eo**ple ____
5. soc**ie**ty ____
6. bel**ie**ve ____
7. qu**ie**t ____
8. s**ui**t ____
9. soc**ia**l ____
10. imm**e**d**ia**te ____
11. z**oo**logy ____
12. z**oo** ____

4. Hearing Stress and Syllables.

In the words below, one of the syllables has primary stress and the others are unstressed. Listen carefully to the words and repeat them slowly. Underline the syllables, cross out any unpronounced vowels, and write the number of syllables in the blank. Mark the stressed syllable. Then write the word under one of the four syllable patterns in the chart below (′ stands for primary stress; ˘ stands for an unstressed syllable).

1. Decémber __3__
2. business ____
3. marriage ____
4. quietly ____
5. problem ____
6. compare ____
7. interesting ____
8. correction ____
9. general ____
10. unable ____
11. believe ____
12. awakened ____
13. police ____
14. national ____
15. arrive ____
16. president ____

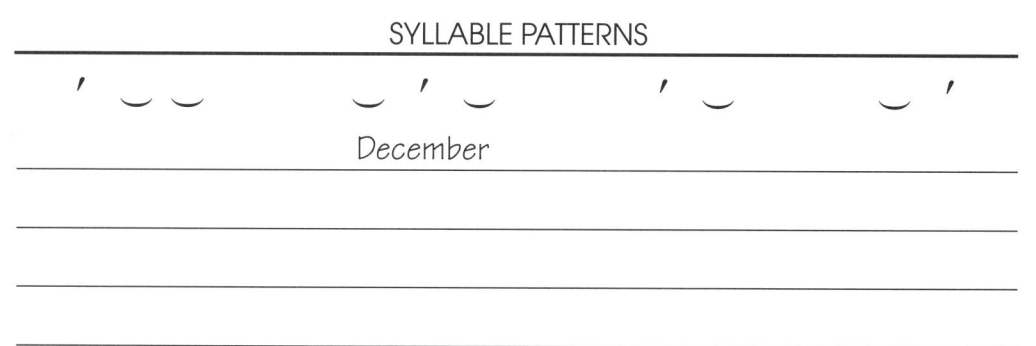

SYLLABLE PATTERNS

′ ˘ ˘   ˘ ′ ˘   ′ ˘   ˘ ′

December

Related Units ▶ 6, 7, 8, 10, 14, 15, 16, 18, 22, 24, 26, 31, 32, 33, 34

UNIT  6

RHYTHM AND INTONATION

Rhythm

Rhythm is the patterning of strong and weak (stressed and unstressed) syllables. Content words (nouns, verbs, adjectives, and adverbs) are usually pronounced more strongly than grammar or function words (articles, helping verbs, short prepositions, personal pronouns, and some conjunctions).

In poetry, rhythm patterns are often repeated and are easy to hear. Rhythm patterns are sometimes repeated in normal speaking, too.

Listen to the rhythm in the lines of poetry and in the dialogue (′ means a strong/stressed syllable; ˘ means a weak/unstressed syllable).

'Twas the night before Christmas, when all through the house,

Not a creature was stirring, not even a mouse.

A: The sofa looks a little tattered.

B: We can't afford to buy a new one.

Practice

1. Hearing Rhythm.   Listen to the dialogue. Mark strong syllables with ′ and weak syllables with ˘. Then practice reading the dialogue with a partner.

A: I told you to throw it.

B: I thought you said kick it.

A: We're not playing soccer.

B: Well, I didn't know that!

Timing Stressed Syllables

Speaking does not usually repeat rhythm patterns the way poetry does, but it is still rhythmic. To keep speech smooth and rhythmic, time the strong beats (stressed syllables) to occur at relatively equal intervals.

Listen to the sentences. Each one has three stressed or strong syllables, but different numbers of unstressed or weak syllables. Even though the number of unstressed syllables is different, the strong syllables are still evenly spaced.

Cláss	stárts	nów.	(3 syllables)
The cláss	is stárting	todáy.	(7 syllables)
The clásses	should be stárting	tomórrow.	(10 syllables)

Although unstressed syllables are weaker, they must still be heard. Do not speak so quickly that you lose sounds or syllables. It is better to lengthen stressed syllables than to rush through unstressed syllables.

Weak or Reduced Words

The vowels and sometimes consonants of some function words are reduced in normal conversation. In informal writing, for example, you may see the word *and* spelled *'n'* : bread *'n'* *water*. The informal spelling shows the normal pronunciation of *and* in speaking: the vowel is reduced to [ə] and the final *-d* is dropped.

Practice

2. Listen carefully to the word-list and reduced (normal speaking) pronunciations of some function words. Is the vowel different? Are consonants lost? Describe the difference.

WORD-LIST PRONUNCIATION	REDUCED (NORMAL SPEAKING) PRONUNCIATION
1. and	red and yellow (*red and* sounds like *redden*)
2. or	read or write (*read or* sounds like *reader*)
3. he	Did he call? (*did he* sounds like *diddy*)
4. can	we can go (*we can* sounds like *weaken*)
5. to	to Ledo (*to Ledo* sounds like *Toledo*)
6. for	for bidding (*for bidding* sounds like *forbidding*)

Thought Groups and Joining

Breaking a sentence into shorter phrases that express a thought helps keep rhythm smooth. There are no fixed rules for dividing a sentence into thought groups. However, some phrases are commonly grouped together. For example, an article and a noun are rarely separated. Usually meaning and sentence length determine what words go together. When you are learning English, you should use short thought groups.

Thought groups are combined into breath groups and pronounced on the same breath. Pauses, where you can take a breath, are usually marked by punctuation (a period, comma, etc.).

Words within a thought group are joined together, without breaks. You can hear the joining most easily when one word ends in a consonant and the next begins with a vowel.

Listen to the different ways of grouping the words in these sentences. Notice how the words are joined together (thought groups are shown by long underlines; joinings are shown by short underlines).

His_uncle lives_on Carter Street.   His_uncle lives_on Carter Street.

Practice

3. Listen and repeat the phrases. Then mark thought groups in sentence 6 and read it out loud. Speak clearly and make joinings.

1. an_apple
2. an_apple_a day
3. the doctor

4. the doctor_away
5. keeps the doctor_away
6. An_apple_a day keeps the doctor_away.

Highlighting Important Words

In a sentence, one word is usually more important than the others and is highlighted by being pronounced on a higher pitch. The most important word often expresses the new information of the sentence.

Listen to the examples.

The **drive** to Springfield takes over ten hours. (not the flight)

The drive to Springfield takes over **ten** hours. (not twenty hours)

Practice

4. The Highlighting Game. Play this game in pairs. A and B are spies who meet in a factory to exchange information. They are standing next to a steam pipe. Every time A tries to tell B some information, a burst of steam comes hissing out of the pipe and B doesn't hear a word clearly (the word is in parentheses, following A's information). B repeats what she thinks she has heard, using rising intonation. A then repeats the correct word, highlighting it with high pitch. A then continues to give B more information. When A is finished, A and B change roles and B gives A information. (A's information is on page 149; B's information is on page 152.) Listen to the example.

Example: A: *The plans are hidden in the p——hissssssss.   (pipe)*

B: *(pie?)* ___Did you say "pie"?___

A: *In the pipe. Go to the house on T——hisssssssss Street.   (Tanner Street)*

B: *(Tanning Street?)* ___Did you say "Tanning Street"?___

A: *Tanner Street. Exactly at f——hissssssss o'clock.   (five o'clock)*

B: *(four o'clock?)* ___Did you say "four o'clock"?___

A: *Five o'clock. Bring a c——hisssssssss.   (camera)*

B: *(candle?)* ___Did you say "candle"?___

A: *A camera.*

Intonation

Intonation is the melody of speech, the pattern of high and low notes. Certain intonation patterns are often used with certain types of sentences. *Yes-no* questions, for example, typically end with a rising intonation. Information questions, on the other hand, typically end with a falling intonation.

Listen to these two questions.

Are you from Brazil?   Where are you from?

Intonation shows the attitude and feeling of the speaker and has an important effect on meaning. Flat or monotone intonation, for example, can mean that the speaker is uninterested, bored, or unhappy.

🎧 Listen to the two readings of this sentence. How does the speaker feel about the chair?

Who bought this chair?   Who bought this chair?

Practice

🎧 **5. Listening.**   Jack and Sylvia are going to have their first vacation in three years. Jack has made a list of possibilities and he is reading them to Sylvia. Sylvia doesn't answer Jack with real words, but her intonation tells him how she feels about his suggestions. As you listen, write down whether you think Sylvia feels enthusiastic, lukewarm, or unenthusiastic about the suggestions.

Jack: A camping trip?   (Sylvia feels _____)

Jack: A fishing trip?   (Sylvia feels_____)

Jack: Renting a house on the ocean?   (Sylvia feels _____)

Jack: A month in New York City?   (Sylvia feels _____)

Jack: A trip to Hawaii?   (Sylvia feels _____)

Jack: Two weeks in Paris?   (Sylvia feels _____)

Related Units ▶ 5, 7, 8, 9, 10, 11, 12, 13, 14, 15, 16, 17, 18, 19, 21, 23, 24, 26, 27, 28, 29, 30, 31, 32, 33, 34, 35, 36, 37, 38, 39, 40

PART II

Basic Features in Pronunciation

- Vowels and Vowel Contrasts
- Consonants
- Stress, Rhythm, and Intonation

UNIT 7

VOWEL CONTRASTS: [iy] AND [ɪ]

■ [iy] is the vowel in *leave*.

When the [iy] vowel is followed by another vowel, join the [y] of [iy] to the next vowel to make a new syllable.

radi^yo   see^ya movie   the^yapple

The -*y* ending in words like *rainy*, *funny*, and *study* is pronounced [iy]. When the next sound is a vowel, join the [y] of [iy] to the vowel.

study‿ing   funny‿ending

■ [ɪ] is the vowel in *give*.

The vowel in *give* is a little shorter than the vowel in *leave*, but the most important difference is the difference in sound quality. ([ɪ] is not just a short version of [iy]; it has a different sound.)

To make [ɪ], start with the vowel in *leave*, and then let your tongue drop down and back a little to make the vowel in *give*. When you make [ɪ], the inside of your mouth should feel very relaxed. [ɪ] is called a "lax" vowel.

Spelling and other details

▶ **[iy]**

ee:	**need, feet, succeed, see**
ie:	bel**ie**ve, p**ie**ce, mov**ie**
ei:	rec**ei**ve
ea:	m**ea**n, **ea**st, r**ea**d (present tense)
i:	pol**i**ce, magaz**i**ne, mach**i**ne, sk**i**

Other spellings: **people, key, medium**

▶ **[ɪ]**

i (followed by a final consonant or two consonants): **kid, sit, rich, listen**

Other spellings: w**o**men, b**u**sy, business,* gym, b**ui**ld, g**ui**lty, g**i**ve, l**i**ve

Business is pronounced as a two-syllable word: bus*i*ness. The letter *i* is not pronounced.

Practice

1. LISTEN AND PRACTICE. Listen to the speaker alternate between [iy] and [ɪ]. Then do the same thing. For [ɪ], let your tongue drop back and down a little and keep your mouth very relaxed.

[iyɪ iyɪ iyɪ iyɪ iyɪ]

2. LISTEN AND PRACTICE. Listen and repeat the words with [iy]. Then choose five and say them out loud. The [iy] vowel ends in a [y] sound that is sometimes hard to hear. Try to make the [y] sound.

1. **E**	3. **need**	5. **seem**	7. **pie**ce
2. b**e**	4. p**eo**ple	6. **lea**ve	8. k**ee**p

3. LISTEN AND PRACTICE. Listen and repeat the words with [ɪ]. Then choose five and say them out loud. Think about saying the vowel in *eat*, and then let your tongue drop back and down a little. Keep your mouth very relaxed.

1. b**i**g	3. l**i**ve	5. b**u**sy	7. w**o**men
2. m**i**ddle	4. m**i**nute	6. th**i**s	8. ch**i**ldren

4. HEARING DIFFERENCES. Listen and repeat the pairs of words with [iy] and [ɪ]. Listen again and circle the word you hear. Then choose three pairs and say them out loud.

1. a. eat	3. a. hill	5. a. reason	7. a. deed
b. it	b. heel	b. risen	b. did
2. a. still	4. a. ship	6. a. leave	8. a. itch
b. steal	b. sheep	b. live	b. each

5. SENTENCES.
Listen to the sentences. Mark thought groups and joinings. Then choose two sentences and read them out loud slowly. Words in the same thought group should be pronounced together.

1. The children did it.
2. I live in this building.
3. The women are swimming in the middle of the river.
4. In a minute, Miss Linn will begin to sing.

6. SOUNDS AND SPELLING.
Listen to the words and say them softly to yourself. Think about the vowel. Write words that have the [iy] vowel in Column A. Write words that have the [ɪ] vowel in Column B. Write words that have a different vowel—not [iy] or [ɪ]—in Column C.

1. live	5. bead	9. guide	13. been
2. alive	6. bread	10. build	14. deep
3. rhythm	7. police	11. medium	15. either
4. rhyme	8. ice	12. medicine	16. their

A: [iy]	B: [ɪ]	C: NOT [iy] OR [ɪ]
	live	

Look at the words in Practice 6 and in the Spelling section on page 22. In a notebook, make a list of any words whose pronunciation surprised you.

7. MEANING DIFFERENCES.

Work in pairs. Take turns asking for definitions of the words with [iy] and [ɪ]. Pronounce the word carefully so your partner knows which definition to choose.

Example: *What does* _____"leave"_____ *mean?*

_____"Leave" means the opposite of "stay."_____

1. a. leave: the opposite of stay
   b. live: the opposite of die

2. a. rich: wealthy
   b. reach: to extend the arm to get something

3. a. ship: a large boat
   b. sheep: a woolly animal

4. a. fill: to put things in a container
   b. feel: to touch something

8. JOINING.

In the words below, the underlined [iy] vowel is followed by another vowel. Listen to the words and write a small *y* between the [iy] vowel and the next vowel to show joining. Then choose four and say them out loud.

1. r a d i ʸo
2. p i a n o
3. r a i n y a f t e r n o o n
4. r e a l i z e
5. i d e a
6. s e e i t
7. b e a d o c t o r
8. s e r i o u s
9. v i d e o

9. QUESTIONS AND ANSWERS.

Ask a *Why* question about one of the sentences below. Choose a classmate to answer it. Be sure to join the verb *be* to the following article *a/an*.

Example: A: *Why* _____is Amy taking art classes_____ ?

B: _____She wants to be a painter_____ .

1. Amy is taking art classes.
2. Akiko is studying photography.
3. Jim is in medical school.
4. Sonia is taking gymnastics classes.
5. Jose is taking physics classes.
6. Ginny is taking dance classes.
7. Eva is in law school.
8. Dick is studying computers.

10. INTERVIEWS. Interview a classmate about his or her job or profession. Read the two questions and write another question of your own.

1. Do you have a job now?

2. What did you want to be when you were young? (Answer with *be a/an . . . .*)

3. _____ ?

In pairs, take turns interviewing your partner and writing down your partner's answers. Then report your information to the class. Speak as clearly and smoothly as you can.

Homework

1. Record the words in Practices 2, 3, and 8.

2. Make a one-minute recording describing what you wanted to be when you were young. Use *be a/an . . . .* Talk about what you are doing now and your plans or goals for the future.

Related Units ▶ 3, 5, 8, 28

UNIT  8

VOWEL CONTRASTS: [ey], [ε], AND [ɪ]

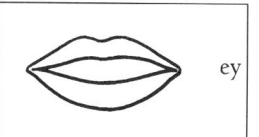

▪ [ey] is the vowel in *wait*, *age*, and *eight*.

[ey] is a tense vowel. Your tongue is toward the front of your mouth and high, but not as high as for [iy], the vowel in *leave*. Your lips are spread when you say [ey].

[ey] is not a "pure" vowel. It ends in a [y] sound. You can easily hear the [y] sound when [ey] is followed by another word that starts with a vowel. It is very important to pronounce the [y] clearly. The [y] helps keep [ey] different from [ε].

stay_open   way_out   say_it

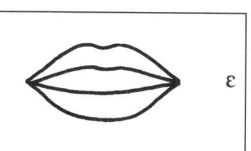

▪ [ε] is the vowel *wet*, *many*, and *head*. [ε] is a relaxed vowel and your lips should not be spread. Your tongue should be a little farther back and lower than it is for [ey].

▪ [ɪ] is the vowel in *wit*, *mix*, and *hid*. It is a relaxed vowel like [ε], but the tongue is a little higher in the mouth.

Spelling and other details

▶ [ey]

aCe ("C" is a consonant; *e* is silent): face, name, make

ai, ay: wait, rain, mail, day, play, say

Other spellings

ein, eig: rein, eight, neighbor

ey: they, convey

ea: break, great

aC(C) (the letter *a* is followed by one or more consonants): table, change, taste

▶ [ε]

eC(C) (the letter *e* is followed by one or more consonants): let, get, never, egg, best

air: chair, hair, air

ead: bread, head, ready

Other spellings

ai: again, said, against

ea: breakfast, heavy, weather

▶ [ɪ] See Unit 7.

1. LISTEN AND PRACTICE. Listen and repeat the words with [ey]. Then choose four and say them out loud. Pronounce the [y] ending of [ey].

1. ate	4. wait	7. late	10. space	13. play
2. age	5. make	8. name	11. date	14. gray
3. break	6. afraid	9. weight	12. safe	15. favor

2. LISTEN AND PRACTICE. Listen and repeat the words with [ε]. Then choose four and say them out loud. Keep the sound relaxed, toward the center of your mouth.

1. healthy	4. wet	7. said	10. friend	13. heavy
2. met	5. send	8. best	11. well	14. pepper
3. breakfast	6. egg	9. guess	12. question	15. bread

3. HEARING DIFFERENCES. Listen and repeat the pairs of words with [ε] and [ɪ]. Listen again and circle the word you hear. Then choose four pairs and say them out loud. Both vowels are relaxed. The tongue should be a little higher for [ɪ] than for [ε].

1. a. Sid	3. a. set	5. a. beg	7. a. bitter
b. said	b. sit	b. big	b. better
2. a. pin	4. a. hair	6. a. fill	8. a. led
b. pen	b. hear	b. fell	b. lid

4. HEARING DIFFERENCES. Listen and repeat the sets of words with [ey], [ε], and [ɪ]. Listen again and circle the word you hear. Then choose two sets and say them out loud. Pronounce the [y] of [ey]. Keep your mouth relaxed for [ε] and [ɪ], but keep your tongue a bit higher for [ɪ].

1. a. mate	4. a. sail
b. met	b. sell
c. mitt	c. sill
2. a. pain	5. a. H
b. pen	b. etch
c. pin	c. itch
3. a. late	6. a. takes
b. let	b. Tex
c. lit	c. ticks

🎧 **5. BINGO.** Listen to each word and write the vowel symbol [ey], [ɛ], or [ɪ] below it. Repeat the words. Then listen again and cross out each word you hear. When you have a complete row or column crossed out, shout out "Bingo!"

1. pain [ey]	5. edge	9. sailor	13. mitt	17. pen
2. met	6. fill	10. pin	14. fell	18. wet
3. lit	7. wait	11. hair	15. let	19. mate
4. age	8. late	12. fail	16. hear	20. seller

🎧 **6. LISTENING.** Make sure you understand the vocabulary and the questions below. Then listen to the story about Jesse James and answer the questions.

band of outlaws	daring crimes	innocent	raider
betray	dust	legend	reward
carry out a plan	gang	mourn	stagecoach

1. When did Jesse James live?
2. What did he and his band of outlaws do?
3. How did he die?
4. Why is he a legend?

🎧 **7. SENTENCES.** Make sure you understand the vocabulary below.

storm	dust	steadily	outlaw	patiently	speck

Now listen and repeat the sentences. Write the correct vowel symbol in the square brackets ([ ]) above the bold-faced letters. Practice saying the sentences to yourself and underline thought groups that are comfortable for you to read. Then choose a sentence and read it out loud.

            [ey] [ɪ]   [ɛ]
1. The summer storm came in from the West and began suddenly.

        [ ]   [ ]   [ ] [ ]   [ ] [ ]
2. When the first heavy drops of rain came down, they raised
    [ ]
little clouds of dust in the dry road.

(continued on next page)

      [ ]   [ ] [ ]

3. Then it began to **rain** steadily.

     [ ] [ ]   [ ]   [ ] [ ]

4. **Jesse James**, the most **famous** outlaw in the **West**, **didn't** seem to mind.

      [ ] [ ]   [ ]   [ ]   [ ]

5. He **waited** patiently for the **message** his brother had **said** he would send.

     [ ]   [ ]   [ ]

6. In the distance, he saw a dark **speck**, growing larger as it **came** toward him.

(S) **8. SPEAKING.**   Listen to the phrases below. Pay attention to the joinings. Then say the phrases out loud.

1. day‿after day   3. pay‿a ransom   5. stay‿away

2. stay‿out‿of sight   4. way‿of life   6. play‿a dangerous game

With a partner, complete the story in Practice 7. What was the dark speck coming toward Jesse James? What did Jesse think it was? How did he feel? What happened when it reached him? Try to use some of the phrases above. Then tell your story to the class.

Homework

1. Record the words in Practices 1, 2, and 5.

2. Tell the story of Jesse James and record it. Include the phrases below and pronounce the vowels carefully. You can add to the story using your imagination or information from an encyclopedia.

   outlaw after the Civil War
   led a gang of outlaws
   trail of robberies and murder through the central states
   betrayed by a member of his gang
   killed for the reward money

Related Units ▶ 3, 7, 9, 12

UNIT 9

VOWEL CONTRASTS: [æ] AND [ɛ]

◾ [æ] is the vowel in *happy, bad,* and *laugh.*

When you make [æ], your mouth should be open and your lips should be spread. Keep the tip of the tongue behind your bottom teeth. The tongue pushes down and front in the mouth.

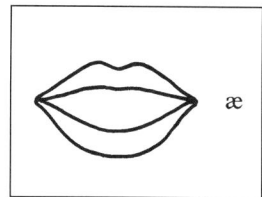

◾ Compare the pictures of [ɛ] and [æ]. Your mouth is open wider when you say [æ].

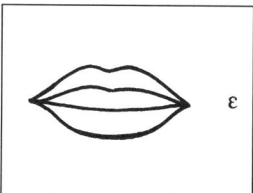 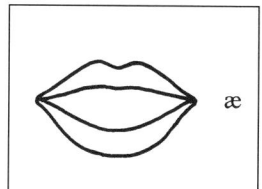

Spelling and other details

▶ [æ]

   a: glad, hat, plastic, valuable, rather

Other spellings

   au: laugh

   ai: plaid

▶ [ɛ] See Unit 8.

1. LISTEN AND PRACTICE. Listen and repeat the words with [æ]. Then choose five and say them out loud.

1. black	4. matter	7. hat	10. exactly
2. relax	5. answer	8. happen	11. plant
3. bad	6. grass	9. magic	12. national

2. HEARING DIFFERENCES. Listen and repeat the pairs of words with [æ] and [ɛ]. Listen again and circle the word you hear. Then choose three pairs and say them out loud.

1. a. bath	3. a. laughed	5. a. gas	7. a. axe
b. Beth	b. left	b. guess	b. X
2. a. past	4. a. sat	6. a. bad	8. a. sad
b. pest	b. set	b. bed	b. said

3. SENSE OR NONSENSE? Listen and repeat the words. All of the words have the [æ] vowel. Make sure you understand the meaning of the words.

A	B	C	D	E	F	G
magic	lad	rat	black	glass	hat	grabbed
happy	hand	bat	plastic	salad	cat	passed
bad	jacket	apple	valuable	gas	stamp	laughed at
laughing	van	man	plaid	cash	banker	cracked

Now work in pairs to complete sentences. Student A's sentence is on page 149 and Student B's sentence is on page 152. Do not show your sentence to your partner. Student A will ask Student B to choose words from the columns above to complete the sentence. Both students can read the sentence out loud and decide if it makes sense. Then Student A will complete Student B's sentence.

Example: A: *Choose a word from Columns A, C, G, and F.*

B: *I choose* _____happy, rat, grabbed, banker_____.

A: *Here is the sentence you made: "The* __happy__ (A) __rat__ (C) __grabbed__ (G) *the* __banker__ (F)*." Does this sentence make sense?*

4. SENSE.

Go back to the sentences on pages 149 and 152 and try to complete them so they make sense. Use the words from Practice 3.

Example: The ___happy___ ___man___ ___laughed at___ the ___cat___ .
               A   C   G   F

5. MEANING DIFFERENCES.

Work in pairs. Read a sentence to your partner. Include either the [æ] or [ɛ] word. Pronounce the word carefully so your partner knows which response to choose. Then switch roles.

Example: I'm afraid I lost the ((bet)/ bat).

        a. Now we won't be able to play baseball!

    (b.) How much money are you out?

1. That's an unusual (axe / X).
   a. Yes, it looks more like a T.
   b. It's from my collection of antique tools.

2. After I told him the story, he (left / laughed).
   a. It was a very funny story.
   b. He had a doctor's appointment.

3. I need a (tan / ten).
   a. I think you look just fine the way you are.
   b. Well, don't ask me for it — you still owe me $20 from last week.

4. I'm afraid my (pen / pan) is no good.
   a. Another excuse not to cook!
   b. Another excuse not to write that letter!

6. EXPANDING VOICE RANGE.

Have you ever been late for school or work and had to make up an excuse? Listen and repeat the excuses below. Use high pitch and strong stress on the important words.

1. My dad fixed a bad salad last night.

2. A black cat crossed my path.

3. My roommate's band was practicing last night.

4. I ran out of gas.

5. The calf got out of the pasture.

6. A tan van crashed into my bicycle.

(continued on next page)

Now imagine that you are late and have to think of an excuse quickly. Make up an excuse using some [æ] words and tell the class your story. You can use one of the excuses above and add to it, or make up your own. Use intonation to make your excuse convincing.

Example: *Late? Why am I late? Oh, well, I have a good explanation for that!*
My dad fixed a BAD salad last night and I
got really sick!

Homework

1. Record the words in Practices 1 and 2.

2. Make up a story using ten of the words from Practice 3. Record your story.

Related Units ▶ 3, 8, 12, 35

UNIT 10

THE MOST COMMON VOWEL: [ə]

■ [ə] is the vowel in *mother, cup,* and *country.*

[ə] is pronounced with the mouth almost closed.

In many words, unstressed vowels are reduced to a short [ə] sound. This makes [ə] the most common vowel sound in English.

[ə] has a special name: It is called *schwa.*

English-speakers sometimes use the schwa sound by itself in a sentence when they need time to think. When used this way, it is spelled *uh.*

> I can't remember where the restaurant is.
> It's . . . uh . . . uh . . . I think it's on State Street.

Spelling and other details

▶ There are many spellings of the vowel sound [ə]. It is often spelled with a *u* between consonants.

  u: cut, cup, luck, run, sun, sudden, dull, jump, hungry, stuff

Other spellings

  o: money, some, love, once, government, discover

  ou: country, tough, enough, touch, trouble, young

  oe: does, doesn't

  a: what, was

  oo: blood, flood

▶ Sometimes the same letter has different vowel sounds.

  o: monkey, done, one [ə]   donkey [ɑ] alone, stone [ow]

  ou: rough [ə]   (al)though [ow] through [uw]   bought, sought [ɔ]

  oo: flood, blood [ə]   food, mood [uw] good, wood, hood [ʊ]

▶ Sometimes different letters have the same vowel sound.

  o, u: son, sun [ə]

  u, ou: us, jealous [ə]

1. LISTEN AND PRACTICE. Listen and repeat the words with [ə]. Then choose six and say them out loud. Keep your mouth almost closed when you say this vowel.

1. son	4. number	7. country	10. dumb
2. once	5. wasn't	8. doesn't	11. money
3. love	6. jump	9. cup	12. blood

2. LISTEN AND PRACTICE. Listen and repeat the phrases with [ə]. Then choose six and say them out loud.

1. a summer Sunday	4. my youngest brother	7. What does he do?
2. enough money	5. a sudden flood	8. funny stuff
3. a hungry buffalo	6. double trouble	9. a loving mother

3. SOUNDS AND SPELLING. Listen to the pairs of words below. The first word has the [ə] vowel. Write *same* if the second word has the same vowel. Write *different* if the second word has a different vowel. Then choose three pairs that are the same, and three pairs that are different, and say them out loud.

1. what, hat _____different_____

2. flood, foot _____

3. country, count _____

4. sun, son _____

5. luck, lock _____

6. tough, though _____

7. cut, company _____

8. one, won _____

9. done, bone _____

10. rush, touch _____

4. SENTENCES. Listen and repeat the sentences. Notice that in sentence 3, the *h* of *he* is lost and *was he* is pronounced exactly like *Wuzzy* (see also Unit 27). Concentrate on joining words and speaking smoothly. Then choose a sentence and say it out loud. Bold-faced letters have the [ə] vowel.

1. Fuzzy Wuzzy was a bear.

2. Fuzzy Wuzzy had no hair.

3. Fuzzy Wuzzy wasn't very fuzzy, was he?

5. REDUCTIONS AND STRESS.
Listen to the words below. The unstressed vowels are all reduced to the [ə] sound. Write the stress symbol ′ below the stressed vowel and [ə] below the unstressed vowel.

1. garden
   <u> ′ </u> <u>ə</u>

2. personal

   __ __ __

3. contain

   __ __

4. apply

   __ __

5. moment

   __ __

6. travel

   __ __

7. private

   __ __

8. open

   __ __

9. produce (verb)

   __ __

6. SENSE OR NONSENSE?
Listen and repeat the words. All of the words have the [ə] vowel. Make sure you understand the meaning of the words.

A	B	C	D	E	F	G	H	I
suddenly	summer	brother	cup	cut	buffalo	tough	much	money
once	month	mother	gun	hug	monkey	hungry	enough	stuff
	Monday	husband	drum	trust	truck	young		honey
		uncle	thumb	hunt	duck	dull		luck
		cousin	stomach	love	bunny	lucky		dust
		mugger		touch		lovely		gum
		hunter				fuzzy		

Now work in pairs to complete sentences. Student A's sentence is on page 149 and Student B's sentence is on page 152. Do not show your sentence to your partner. Student A will ask Student B to choose words from the columns above to complete the sentence. Both students can read the sentence out loud and decide if it makes sense. Then Student A will complete Student B's sentence.

Example: A: *Choose a word from Column F, two from Column G, one from Column E, one from Column A, one from Column I, one from Column D, and another from Column E.*

B: *I choose* <u>truck, lucky, young, hunt, once, dust, gun, love</u>.

A: *Here is the sentence you made: "My baby* <u>truck</u> *s were very*
F

<u>lucky</u> *. They were so* <u>young</u> *to* <u>hunt</u> *.* <u>Once</u>
G   G   E   A

I put some <u>dust</u> *in a* <u>gun</u> *. They* <u>love</u> *(e)d it."*
I   D   E

Does this sentence make sense?

7. SENSE.   Go back to the sentences on pages 149 and 152 and try to complete them so they make sense. Use the words from Practice 6.

Example: "*My baby* _duck_ *s were very* _fuzzy_ *. They were*
            F   G

so _lovely_ *to* _touch_ *.* _Once_ *I put some* _honey_
       G   E   A   I

in a _cup_ *. They* _love_ *(e)d it."*
           D   E

Homework

1. Record the phrases in Practice 2 and the word pairs in Practice 3.

2. Write a short story using words from Practice 6. Record your story.

Related Units ▶ 3, 5, 11, 12, 13, 27, 31, 32, 33, 35, 36, 37, 38

UNIT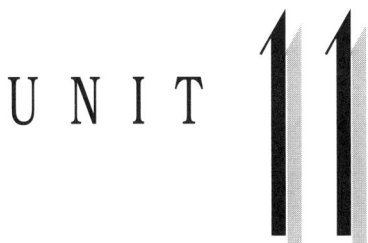

VOWEL CONTRASTS: [ɑ] AND [ə]

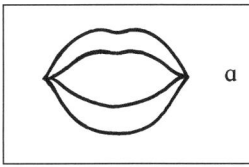

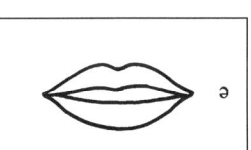

▪ [ɑ] is the vowel in *not, shop,* and *possible.*

[ɑ] is pronounced in the middle of the mouth. The mouth is very open.

▪ [ə] is the vowel in *nut, gun,* and *much.*

[ə] is also pronounced in the middle of the mouth, but the mouth is almost closed. This vowel has a special name: schwa.

Spelling and other details

▶ [ɑ] is usually spelled with the letter *o* between consonants.

hot, not, lock, possible, Don, shot, rob, stop

Other spellings

a: want, father, watch, car, start, hard, charge

ua: guard

▶ [ə] See Unit 10.

 ▰▰▰▰▰▰▰▰▰▰ Practice ▰▰▰▰▰▰▰▰

1. LISTEN AND PRACTICE. Listen and repeat the words with [ɑ]. Then choose five and say them out loud. Your mouth should be open.

1. rob	4. collar	7. odd	10. problem
2. shot	5. dock	8. block	11. box
3. soccer	6. modern	9. popular	12. solid

2. MOUTH SHAPES. Listen and repeat the phrases with [ɑ] and [ə]. Then choose four from each column and say them out loud. In the first column, the first word has the open vowel [ɑ] and the second word has the closed vowel [ə]. In the second column, the first word has the closed vowel [ə] and the second word has the open vowel [ɑ].

OPEN [ɑ] - CLOSED [ə]	CLOSED [ə] - OPEN [ɑ]
1. hot cup	8. tough job
2. not enough	9. one block
3. stop suddenly	10. double lock
4. modern country	11. young father
5. popular government	12. come on
6. hot summer	13. lucky lottery winner
7. rotten luck	14. hungry hogs

3. SENTENCES. These sentences contain phrases from Practice 2. Listen to the sentences and write the vowel symbol ([ɑ] or [ə]) above the bold-faced letters. Underline thought groups. Then choose two sentences and say them out loud.

     [ə]   [ɑ] [ɑ]
1. I have a **do**uble l**o**ck **o**n my door.

     [ ] [ ] [ ]
2. She lives **o**ne bl**o**ck fr**o**m the school.

     [ ] [ ]
3. Learning a new language is a **tou**gh j**o**b.

     [ ]   [ ][ ]
4. The driver st**o**pped the b**u**s s**u**ddenly.

     [ ]   [ ] [ ]
5. The c**u**p is too h**o**t to t**ou**ch.

     [ ] [ ]   [ ]   [ ]   [ ] [ ]
6. The farmer has **o**ne d**o**nkey, two m**o**nkeys, and a h**u**ndred h**u**ngry h**o**gs.

4. HEARING DIFFERENCES. Listen and repeat the pairs of words with [ɑ] and [ə]. Listen again and circle the word you hear. Then choose four pairs and say them out loud.

1. a. once	3. a. shot	5. a. collar	7. a. duck	9. a. luck
b. wants	b. shut	b. color	b. dock	b. lock
2. a. box	4. a. rub	6. a. soccer	8. a. hot	10. a. cup
b. bucks	b. rob	b. succor	b. hut	b. cop

🎧 **5. BINGO.** Listen to each word. Write *open* under the [ɑ] words and *closed* under the [ə] words. Repeat the words. Then listen again and cross out each word you hear. When you have a complete row or column crossed out, shout out "Bingo!"

1. lock *open*	6. **once**	11. hug	16. cop	21. collar	26. wants
2. socks	7. luck	12. not	17. bucks	22. robber	27. color
3. cut	8. shot	13. box	18. duck	23. shut	28. body
4. nut	9. rubber	14. buddy	19. hut	24. sucks	29. cot
5. hog	10. Don	15. cup	20. dock	25. done	30. hot

6. MEANING DIFFERENCES. Work in pairs. Ask your partner a question. Include either the [ɑ] or [ə] word. Pronounce the word carefully so your partner knows which response to choose. Then switch roles.

Example: *What's a (hog/(hug))?*

   a. A hog is an adult male pig.

   (b.)A hug is an embrace.

1. What's a (dock/duck)?
   a. A dock is a place where boats can tie up.
   b. A duck is a water bird that goes "quack quack."

2. What's a (cup/cop)?
   a. A cup is a drinking container for hot drinks.
   b. A cop is a police officer.

(continued on next page)

3. What's (succor/soccer)?
    a. Succor is a formal word for "help."
    b. Soccer is the most popular sport in the world.

4. What's a (knot/nut)?
    a. A knot is what you get when you tie two pieces of rope or string together.
    b. A nut is a small food that is inside a shell.

Homework

1. Record the words and phrases in Practices 1 and 2.

2. Write a short story about a cop and a robber. Record the story. Try to include some of the [ɑ] and [ə] words below and pronounce them correctly.

[ɑ]	[ə]
cop	gun
drop	luck, lucky, unlucky
problem	money
rob, robber, robbery	suddenly
stop	trouble

Related Units ▶ 3, 6, 10, 12

UNIT 12

REVIEW:[ɛ], [æ], [ə], AND [ɑ]

─────────── Practice ───────────

1. LISTEN AND PRACTICE. Listen and repeat the words with [ɛ], [æ], [ə], and [ɑ]. Then choose two rows of words and say them out loud. Concentrate on the shape of your mouth for the different vowels.

 ɛ, beg   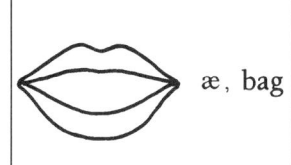 æ, bag   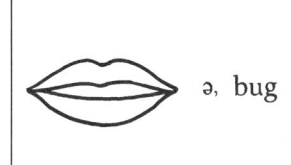 ə, bug   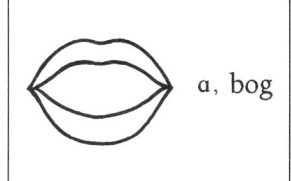 ɑ, bog

1. a. beg	b. bag	c. bug	d. bog
2. a. flex	b. flax	c. flux	d. flocks
3. a. net	b. Nat/gnat	c. nut	d. not/knot
4. a. blender	b. blander	c. blunder	d. blonder
5. a. lest	b. last	c. lust	d. lost
6. a. peppy	b. pappy	c. puppy	d. poppy
7. a. leg	b. lag	c. lug	d. log
8. a. pet	b. pat	c. putt	d. pot
9. a. Tex	b. tax/tacks	c. tucks	d. tocks
10. a. den	b. Dan	c. done	d. Don

2. BINGO.
Listen to each word and write the vowel symbol [ɛ], [æ], [ə], or [ɑ] below it. Repeat the words. Then listen again and cross out each word you hear. When you have a complete row or column crossed out, shout out "Bingo!"

1. lock [ɑ]	6. blonder	11. guest	16. collar
2. blender	7. Don	12. blander	17. gust
3. color	8. lack	13. Keller	18. hum
4. wants	9. gassed	14. ham	19. luck
5. hem	10. blunder	15. done	20. once

3. SENTENCES.
Listen and repeat the sentences. Mark thought groups and joinings. Then choose two sentences and say them out loud.

1. The peppy puppy ate all the poppies.
2. Are Dan and Don done in the den?
3. Nat did not put the nuts in the net.
4. The clock that Tex got goes tick-tock.
5. He lagged behind because he injured his leg on the fallen log.
6. The big black bug bled black blood.
7. Wendy wondered where her wand was.
8. Mr. Black blocked the blond from blending the bran with the blender.

4. MEANING DIFFERENCES. Work in pairs. Read a sentence to your partner. Include one of the words in parentheses. Pronounce the word carefully so your partner knows which response to choose. Then switch roles.

Example: *That (blender /(blunder)) is going to cost a lot!*

  a. Who would think kitchen appliances could be so expensive!

  (b.) *Well, I've warned you about doing things too quickly.*

1. Watch out! There's a (bug/bog) over there!
   a. I'm not afraid of insects.
   b. I've got my boots on.

2. Isn't that a (gnat/nut) in your soup?
   a. How disgusting! Waiter, take this back!
   b. There should be quite a few. It's made with peanuts.

3. What kind of (luck/lock) do you have?
   a. Not very much—I've never won anything in my life.
   b. A really strong one—I'm afraid of burglars.

4. They made a lot of noise when they (left/laughed).
   a. Even the neighbors heard the banging doors.
   b. The movie was really funny.

Homework

Record the words and sentences in Practices 1 and 3.

Related Units ▶ 3, 6, 8, 9, 10, 11

UNIT 13

PRONOUNCING [r] AFTER VOWELS

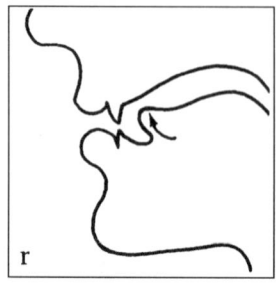

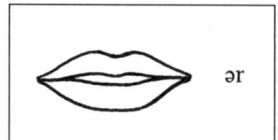

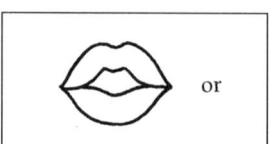

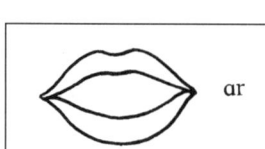

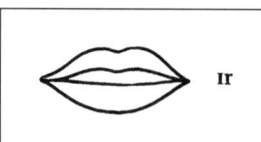

- In most dialects of American English, [r] is pronounced after vowels. To pronounce [r] after a vowel, turn the tip of your tongue up and back.

- The [ər] sound occurs in words like *first*, *her*, and *work*.

  To make [ər], your lips should be almost closed. Inside your mouth, the tip of the tongue turns up and back.

- The [or] sound occurs in words like *more*, *war*, and *four*.

  To make [or], your lips should be rounded. Inside your mouth, the tip of the tongue turns up and back.

- The [ɑr] sound occurs in words like *hard*, *heart*, and *car*.

  To make [ɑr], your mouth should be very open. Inside your mouth, the tip of the tongue turns up and back.

- The [ɪr] sound occurs in words like *here*, *deer*, and *near*.

  To make [ɪr], your lips should be almost closed and spread. Inside your mouth, the tip of the tongue turns up and back.

- The [ɛr] sound occurs in words like *hair*, *wear*, and *bear*.

  To make [ɛr], your mouth should be open a little more than for [ɪr]. Inside your mouth, the tip of the tongue turns up and back.

Spelling and other details

▶ *wor* spellings usually have the [ər] sound: *work, word, worse, worth, worm.*

▶ *war* spellings usually have the [or] sound: *war, warm, ward, warn.*

▶ *ir* and *ur* spellings usually have the [ər] sound: *bird, circle, first, turn, burn, hurt.*

▶ *Hear* and *here* are pronounced the same. *Their* and *there* are pronounced the same. In normal spoken English *they're* is the same as *their/there.*

▶ In some words, an unstressed *e* before *r* is not pronounced. These words look as if they have three syllables, but most English-speakers pronounce them as two-syllable words:

evᴇry   intᴇrest   genᴇral

sevᴇral   tempᴇrature   diffᴇrent

Practice

1. **MOUTH EXERCISES.**   Try to picture the inside of your mouth and the tip of your tongue. Think about them. Without making any sound, touch the top of your mouth with the tip of your tongue. Think about how the tip of the tongue is pointing up and is turned back a little. When you make [r] after a vowel, your tongue is in a similar position, except it does not touch the top of the mouth.

2. **LISTEN AND PRACTICE.**   Listen and repeat the words with [ər]. Then choose six and say them out loud. Keep your lips flat and almost closed. Turn the tip of your tongue up and back.

1. bird	5. turn	9. worse	13. her
2. burn	6. heard	10. first	14. were
3. word	7. hurt	11. serve	15. shirt
4. circle	8. work	12. earth	16. term

3. **LISTEN AND PRACTICE.**   Listen and repeat the words with [or]. Then choose six and say them out loud. Round your lips as you turn the tip of your tongue up and back.

1. tore	5. more	9. door	13. bore
2. sore	6. short	10. warm	14. four
3. war	7. corn	11. floor	15. warn
4. shore	8. formal	12. store	16. ordinary

4. LISTEN AND PRACTICE. Listen and repeat the words with [ɑr]. Then choose six and say them out loud. Your mouth should be open as you turn the tip of your tongue up and back.

1. car	4. hard	7. charge	10. garden
2. start	5. heart	8. sharp	11. guard
3. yard	6. large	9. part	12. mark

5. SOUNDS AND SPELLING. Listen to the pairs of words below. Write *same* if the bold-faced letters in the two words have the same sound. Write *different* if the bold-faced letters in the two words have different sounds. Then choose three pairs that are the same, and three pairs that are different, and say them out loud.

1. here, hear _____same_____

2. were, war _____

3. perfect, pardon _____

4. work, word _____

5. burn, bird _____

6. war, wore _____

7. her, hair _____

8. heard, hard _____

9. hurt, word _____

10. worse, wore _____

11. heard, beard _____

12. worm, warm _____

6. MOUTH SHAPES. Listen to the words below. If the word has the [ər] sound, write it in Column A. If the word has the [or] sound, write it in Column B. If the word has the [ɑr] sound, write it in Column C. Then say the words in each column out loud. Turn the tip of your tongue up and back to make the [r].

1. word	3. war	5. hard	7. heart	9. heard	11. warm
2. large	4. born	6. work	8. her	10. horn	12. guard

A: [ər]	B: [or]	C: [ɑr]
word		

7. PROVERBS AND JOININGS. Make sure you understand the words below. Then listen to the proverbs, mark joinings and thought groups, and repeat the proverbs.

worm	worth	bush	feather	flock
marketing	major	firm	habit	get a raise
get the boot	ambitious			

PROVERBS

1. The early bird gets the worm.

2. A bird in the hand is worth two in the bush.

3. Birds of a feather flock together.

Now listen to the situations. After you listen, work with a partner and match the proverbs with the situations. Write the proverb below the situation it describes.

SITUATIONS

1. Bert and Bart grew up in the same neighborhood in New York City. They went to the same church and to the same school. They liked the same music and the same food. In high school they both fell in love with the same girl. This dangerous situation might have broken up their friendship, but it didn't. The girl was not interested in either Bert or Bart. When Bert and Bart graduated from high school, they decided to go to the same college. Nobody was surprised when they both chose marketing as their major.

   Proverb: _____

2. After college, Bert and Bart both got jobs at the same firm. Although Bert and Bart were alike in many ways, their work habits were very different. Bert came to work early every day. He stayed at work late almost every night. Bart liked to party. He often came late to work. He never once stayed late and he often asked to leave early. After six months, Bert got a raise and Bart got the boot.

   Proverb: _____

(continued on next page)

3. Bart's feelings were not hurt when he got fired. He was an ambitious young man. He began interviewing for other jobs. He was interested in two firms. The first firm offered him a job with good pay. The second firm said, "Maybe—don't call us, we'll call you." Bart thought he could get even more money from the first firm. He told the first firm that the second firm had offered him a job with more money. He also said that he would take the job with the second firm if the first firm wouldn't pay him more money. The first firm said, "Okay, take the other job." Bart's still looking for work.

Proverb: _____

8. **SPEAKING.**   Think of something you learned to do or are learning to do now. Write down two or three sentences about your experience and then tell the class about it. Try to use some of the words below, and speak as smoothly and clearly as you can.

Examples: I learned to ride a bike when I was six. At first, it was really hard, and I fell a lot. But I was determined and I finally learned.

I'm learning to speak English. Sometimes I get really nervous when I have to talk. But I'm determined to speak well. English is important for me professionally.

hard	learn	hurt	worry	nervous
first	later	tired	ever	concerned
exhilarated	discouraged	determined	important	urgent
embarrassed	understand	work	better	future

Homework

1. Record the words in Practices 2, 3, and 4.

2. Make a one-minute recording about your experience learning English or another foreign language. Try to use some of the words from Practice 8.

Related Units ▶ 3, 4, 5, 25

UNIT 14

VOWEL CONTRASTS: [ow], [ɔ], AND [a]

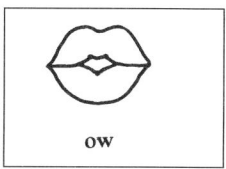

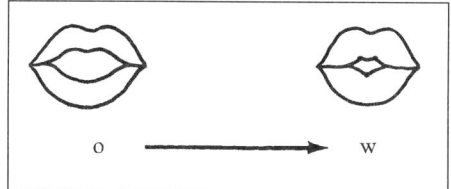

■ [ow] is the vowel in *go, hope,* and *kn**ow**.*

[ow] does not have a pure [o] sound. It ends in a [w] sound. The letter *w*, however, is not often used in spellings of the [ow] vowel. Practice [ow] in front of a mirror to make sure you are pronouncing it correctly. Your lips should be rounded for the [o] sound, and then round even more for the [w] sound. When [ow] is followed by a vowel, be sure to join the [w] to the next vowel.

go͜ʷin co͜ʷoperate show_up I've no͜ʷidea

■ [ɔ] is the vowel in *bought* and *caught.*

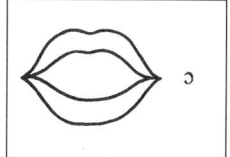

■ [a] is the vowel in *not* and *cot.*

Sometimes [ow] is confused with [ɔ] or [a]. Look at the difference in the mouth diagrams for [ow], [ɔ], and [a]. For [ow], the lips are tightly rounded. For [ɔ], the mouth is open, the tongue is back, and the lips are slightly rounded. For [a], the mouth is wide open and the lips are not rounded.

Many native English-speakers use the [a] vowel instead of [ɔ]. These speakers pronounce *cot* and *caught* with the same vowel—the [a] vowel.

Spelling and other details

▶ [ow]

    o: go, no, hello, open, won't, most, told

    oCe ("C" is a consonant; *e* is silent):
       rode, those, joke, nose, home

    oa: boat, coat, road, soap, toad

    ow: know, show, window, yellow, throw,
       tomorrow

Other spellings

    oe: toe, Joe

    ough: though, dough

    ew: sew

▶ [ɔ]

    o: long, boss, lost, wrong, across

    au: fault, caught, August, audience

    al: tall, salt, also, all, fall

    aw: flaw, draw, law, awful

Other spellings

    ough: thought, bought, brought

    augh: taught, daughter, caught

    oa: broad

▶ [ɑ] See Unit 11.

Practice

1. LISTEN AND PRACTICE. Listen and repeat the words with [ow], [ɑ], and [ɔ]. Then choose three from each column and say them out loud.

[ow]	[ɑ]	[ɔ]
1. coat	8. rob	15. fought
2. frozen	9. shot	16. thought
3. October	10. cop	17. long
4. show	11. rock	18. loss
5. drove	12. stocking	19. caught
6. ago	13. car	20. law
7. home	14. possible	21. crawl

2. JOINING. Listen and repeat the phrases. Mark joinings. If the [w] of [ow] is not part of the spelling, write a small *w* between [ow] and the next sound.

1. no^wapplesauce
2. a row of chairs
3. bow and arrow
4. cooperation
5. throw it away
6. a know-it-all
7. tomorrow afternoon
8. so unfriendly
9. go away
10. yellow and red
11. Croatian
12. a window of opportunity

3. MEANING DIFFERENCES. Work in pairs. Ask your partner a question. Include one of the words in parentheses. Pronounce the word carefully so your partner knows which response to choose. Then switch roles.

> *Example:* *What do you think of this (ⓒⓞⓣ/coat)?*
>
> > a. *It's beautiful and it fits you perfectly!*
> >
> > ⓑ. *Surely we can afford a real bed!*

1. Do you think he was (called/cold)?
   a. I'm sure of it. His lips were blue, and his teeth were chattering.
   b. I'm sure of it. Nancy said she spoke to him last night.

2. What happened? That's a really horrible (score/scar)!
   a. I cut myself.
   b. I didn't study.

3. I really need a (lawn/loan).
   a. You say that every year—why don't you just throw some seed on the ground?
   b. You say that every year—why don't you just go to the bank and apply for one?

🎧 **4. DIALOGUES.** Listen and repeat the words. Make sure you understand them.

1. envious	3. angry	5. unhappy	7. articulate	9. impolite
2. upset	4. uncomfortable	6. odd	8. embarrassed	10. insecure

With a partner, write two dialogues following the example. Use words from the list above. Practice the dialogues, making the joinings and using strong intonation. Speak as clearly as you can. Then perform a dialogue for the class. Listen to the example.

> *Example:* A: *She/he was really___upset___!*
>
> B: *How___upset___ was she/he?*
>
> A: *She/he was so___upset___ that she/he broke the window!*

Homework

1. Record the words and phrases from Practices 1 and 2.

2. Look at the words in Practice 4. Think of a situation where one of the words describes how you felt (for example, *embarrassed*). Make a one-minute recording describing the situation. Include the phrase *so . . . that*, and speak as clearly and smoothly as you can.

Related Units ▶ 3, 5, 7, 11, 12

UNIT 15

VOWEL CONTRASTS: [uw] AND [ʊ]; THE BEGINNING SOUND: [wʊ]

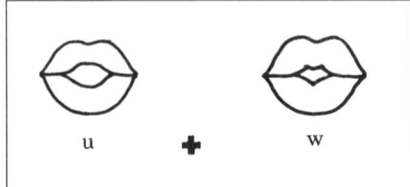

- [uw] is the vowel in *food, rude,* and *do.* [uw] ends in a [w] sound. Your lips should start in the position for [u] and continue rounding to [w].

  When [uw] is followed by a vowel in the same word or in the next word, join the [w] of [uw] to the vowel.

  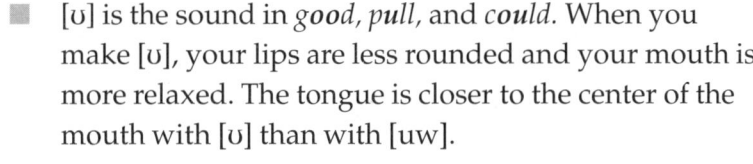

- [ʊ] is the sound in *good, pull,* and *could.* When you make [ʊ], your lips are less rounded and your mouth is more relaxed. The tongue is closer to the center of the mouth with [ʊ] than with [uw].

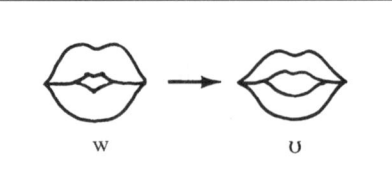

- [wʊ] is the beginning sound of *wood, woman,* and a few other words in English. Some students have difficulty pronouncing the beginning [w] of this sound. When these students say *wood,* their pronunciation may sound more like *'ood.* If this sound is a problem for you, start with your lips very rounded and then unround to the [ʊ] vowel. It is unrounding that creates a beginning [w] sound. Practice this sound slowly in front of a mirror. Make sure you can see and feel the lips unround.

Spelling and other details

▶ [uw]

    oo: **food, cool, noon, choose**

    u: **student, rude, truth, revolution, June**

Other spellings

    o: **do, to, who, move**

    ou: **you, group, through**

    ew: **new, grew, threw**

    ui: **suit, juice**

    eau: **beauty**

▶ [ʊ]

    oo: **good, foot, look, hood**

    u: **put, pull, sugar, push**

Other spellings

    ou: **would, could, should**

    o: **woman**

Practice

1. LISTEN AND PRACTICE.   Listen and repeat the words with [uw] and [ʊ]. Then choose three words with [uw] and three words with [ʊ] and say them out loud.

	[uw]			[ʊ]	
1. June		5. blue		9. book	13. could
2. include		6. soon		10. look	14. cook
3. introduce		7. truth		11. woman	15. sugar
4. fool		8. two		12. put	16. hood

2. HEARING DIFFERENCES.   Listen and repeat the pairs of words with [uw] and [ʊ]. Listen again and circle the word you hear. Then choose four pairs and say them out loud.

1. a. stood		3. a. cooed		5. a. who'd		7. a. Luke	
b. stewed		b. could		b. hood		b. look	
2. a. suit		4. a. should		6. a. pull		8. a. fool	
b. soot		b. shooed		b. pool		b. full	

3. IDIOMS AND EXPRESSIONS.   Listen and repeat the tongue twister. Underline thought groups and mark joinings. Practice reading the tongue twister with a partner, and then do a class reading of it.

How much wood would a woodchuck[1] chuck[2]

If a woodchuck could chuck wood?

Just as much as a woodchuck would

If a woodchuck could chuck wood.

1. woodchuck: a beaver-sized rodent that tunnels in the ground, common in the northeastern United States

2. to chuck: to throw (slang)

4. IDIOMS AND EXPRESSIONS.   Listen and repeat the idioms in Column A. Mark joinings. Match the idioms to the definitions in Column B. Then choose an idiom and ask a classmate to define it, using a complete sentence.

A	B
1. black and blue	a. please oneself
2. sugar and spice	b. an opportunity to enter something
3. pull something off	c. bruised
4. suit oneself	d. little girls are made of this (according to a saying)
5. true to form	e. fight ferociously
6. put up with someone	f. endure, tolerate
7. food for thought	g. following a pattern
8. (have) a foot in the door	h. something to think about
9. fight tooth and nail	i. do something in spite of difficulties

5. DIALOGUES.   With a partner, complete the dialogues using idioms from Practice 4. Mark thought groups and joinings. Then practice reading the dialogues with your partner.

1. A: Was June hurt badly in the accident?

   B: No, she was _____ _____ _____ all over, but she didn't have any broken bones.

2. A: Do you want the mayor to be reelected?

   B: No. We've _____ _____ _____ _____ for four years already and that's enough!

3. A: Do you really think I can get a job with the newspaper?

   B: Well, I'd say you already have _____ _____ _____

   _____ _____ — you're dating the editor's daughter!

56 UNIT 15

4. A: Don't try to talk me out of it! I'm going to buy that sports car!

B: Okay— _____ _____. After all, you have to drive it. But don't forget—you also have to pay for the gas!

6. **SPEAKING.** With a partner, choose one of the situations below and present it to the class. Speak as clearly and smoothly as you can. Try to use some of these expressions.

Asking for advice: Do you think I should . . . ?

Should I . . . ?

Making suggestions, giving advice: If I were you, I'd . . . .

You could . . . .

I (don't) think you should . . . .

1. This weekend you are going to meet your boyfriend's/girlfriend's parents. You are going to their house for dinner. You're very nervous because you want to make a good impression. You're not sure what you should wear, what you should talk about, whether you should bring a gift, and so on. Ask your boyfriend/girlfriend for suggestions.

2. Your roommate's family, who live in Pennsylvania, have invited you to spend the Christmas holidays at their home. You're not familiar with that part of the country or with American customs. You don't know what clothes to bring for the weather (or the holiday), whether you should bring gifts, whether you should offer to help the family with household chores like the dishes, and so on. Ask your roommate for help.

3. Your boss has invited you to dinner at a romantic restaurant this weekend, and you have accepted. You have a feeling that your boss may be interested in you romantically, even though he/she has never done or said anything before. You are very nervous about this dinner. You realize that you really don't know anything about your boss's private life—not even whether he/she is married. This job is important to you, and you don't want to do anything to jeopardize it—still, you do find your boss attractive. You need some advice on what to wear to the dinner, what to talk about, and how to act. Ask your best friend.

Homework

1. Record the words in Practices 1 and 2.

2. Record the tongue twister in Practice 3.

Related Units ▶ 3, 5, 20

UNIT 16

THE THREE DIPHTHONGS: [aw], [ay], AND [oy]

A diphthong is a vowel plus [w] or [y]. English has three diphthongs: [aw], [ay], and [oy].

■ [aw] is the vowel in *house*, *now*, and *cow*.

■ [ay] is the vowel in *die*, *try*, and *ice*.

■ [oy] is the vowel in *boy*, *noise*, and *toy*.

When [aw], [ay], or [oy] is followed by another vowel, join the [w] or [y] to the next vowel.

How‿are you?   Why‿is this here?   The toy‿is broken.

If you are a native speaker of Chinese, you may need to pronounce the [y] of [ay] more strongly, especially when the vowel is followed by a nasal consonant, as in *time* [taym]. If this is a problem for you, pay special attention to the [y] sound in this vowel.

Spelling and other details

▶ [aw]

   ou: house, about, south, thousand

   ow: now, allow, down, crowd

▶ [ay]

   i: ice, decide, child, find

   y: cry, try, by, type

   ie: lie, die, fried

   igh: night, high, sight, frighten

These words have less common spellings of the [ay] vowel: *buy, island,* * *guide, sign, aisle,* * *height, eye, choir*

▶ [oy]

   oy: toy, boy, enjoy, annoy, loyal

   oi: noise, oil, poison, coin

*The s is silent in these words: *island, aisle.*

---

1. LISTEN AND PRACTICE. Listen and repeat the words. Then choose three from each column and say them out loud.

[aw]	[ay]	[oy]
1. m**ou**se	8. s**igh**	15. j**oy**
2. cr**ow**ded	9. t**i**me	16. n**oi**sy
3. t**ow**n	10. r**igh**t	17. ann**oy**
4. sh**ou**t	11. **ai**sle	18. **oi**l
5. l**ou**d	12. **i**sland	19. s**oi**l
6. m**ou**ntain	13. cl**i**mb	20. empl**oy**er
7. p**ou**nd	14. fr**igh**ten	21. l**oy**alty

2. IDIOMS AND EXPRESSIONS. Listen to the sentences and mark the joinings. Then choose a sentence and read it out loud. Guess the meaning of the bold-faced expression in the sentence.

1. I knew you were strong, but it was an **eye-opener** to see you lift the car.

2. I'm pretty comfortable living by myself, but **every now and then** I feel homesick.

3. **How in the world** did he escape from that burning building?

4. Many **child actors** aren't able to continue their career successfully as adults.

5. The new baby is the **joy of their life.**

6. Our neighbor is going to **keep an eye on** our house while we're on vacation.

7. **Why in the world** did you lend him your car? He's a terrible driver!

8. If we don't leave right away, the storm will be here and we won't be able to leave. It's **now or never.**

9. The director is holding **tryouts** for the school play. I'm **trying out** for the main part.

10. Don't try to talk to him now. He's upset with you, and I'm afraid he'll **fly off the handle** when he sees you.

3. LISTENING. Make sure you understand the vocabulary and the questions below. Then listen to "A Bundle of Phobias" and answer the questions.

bundle	phobia	claustrophobic	panicky	spinning	spiders

1. What is a phobia?
2. What is claustrophobia?
3. Mr. Swanson mentions eleven things he is afraid of. What are they? Write down as many as you can.

4. INTERVIEWS. Interview a classmate about his or her fears. Ask about common fears, such as fear of flying, as well as any other fears. Report your information to the class. Speak as clearly and smoothly as you can.

Homework

Record the words and sentences in Practices 1 and 2.

Related Units ▶ 3, 5, 20, 28

UNIT 17

BEGINNING AND FINAL CONSONANTS

🎧 Beginning Voiceless Stop Consonants: [p, t, k]

When a word begins with a voiceless stop consonant followed by a vowel, the stop is pronounced with a strong puff of air called "aspiration" (written ʻ). If you hold a piece of paper in front of your face with the bottom edge about two inches from your mouth and say *pan*, the paper will blow away from your mouth. Listen.

pʻan   tʻwo   cʻome

🎧 Final Voiced and Voiceless Stop Consonants: [b, d, g, p, t, k]

At the end of a word, voiced and voiceless stop consonants are pronounced and held, but are not released strongly (written ʼ). If you release the consonant strongly, the word may sound like it has an extra, unnecessary syllable. Listen.

jobʼ   needʼ   rugʼ   hopʼ   neatʼ   sickʼ

Final stop consonants may be hard to hear because they are not released. The length of the vowel preceding the stop can help you hear the final sound. The vowel before a final voiceless stop will sound "cut off" and short. The vowel before a final voiced stop is also "cut off" but is a little longer. If a word ends in a vowel, the vowel is not cut off at all. Listen.

FINAL VOICELESS STOP (shorter vowel)	FINAL VOICED STOP (longer vowel)	FINAL VOWEL (vowel not "cut off")
make	made	may
late	laid	lay
seek	heed	he

🎧 Other Final Voiced Consonants: [ð, v, z, ʒ, dʒ]

These consonants are also not released strongly at the end of a word. Pronounce the final consonants, but let them "die away" quickly. Listen.

breatheʼ   liveʼ   roseʼ   rougeʼ   edgeʼ

∩ Final Consonants Followed by Vowels

When a word that ends in a consonant is followed by a word that begins with a vowel, join or release the final consonant to the vowel. Listen.

kick‿it   read‿a book   edge‿of the paper

▰▰▰▰▰ Practice ▰▰▰▰▰

(S) **1. LISTEN AND PRACTICE.** Listen and repeat the words. Then choose four and say them out loud. Use strong aspiration with the beginning consonants. Test yourself using a sheet of paper, if you want.

1. kʰey	4. pʰie	7. tʰea
2. pʰen	5. cʰow	8. Tʰom
3. tʰell	6. pʰill	9. cʰame

∩ **2. HEARING FINAL CONSONANTS.** Listen to the words. Circle "final consonant" if you hear a final consonant. Circle "no final consonant" if you do not.

1.	final consonant	no final consonant
2.	final consonant	no final consonant
3.	final consonant	no final consonant
4.	final consonant	no final consonant
5.	final consonant	no final consonant
6.	final consonant	no final consonant
7.	final consonant	no final consonant
8.	final consonant	no final consonant
9.	final consonant	no final consonant

∩ **3. HEARING DIFFERENCES.** Listen and repeat the pairs of words. Listen again and circle the word you hear. Then choose four pairs and say them out loud. Make the vowel before a voiced consonant longer, but do not release final voiced or voiceless consonants.

1. a. hat	4. a. seed	7. a. duck
b. had	b. seat	b. dug
2. a. cab	5. a. state	8. a. pick
b. cap	b. stayed/staid	b. pig
3. a. rope	6. a. said	9. a. log
b. robe	b. set	b. lock

4. APPLYING THE RULE. Listen and repeat the phrases. Mark the bold-faced consonants that are unreleased (use '). Mark the joining if the final consonant is joined to a vowel. Then choose four phrases and say them out loud. Choose phrases with both unreleased and joined consonants.

1. drug' dealer
2. I love pears
3. find gold
4. job ad
5. read articles

6. job hunting
7. sick and tired
8. drug addict
9. I love apples
10. language course

11. find oil
12. that one
13. sick today
14. read newspapers
15. language ability

5. LISTENING. Make sure you understand the vocabulary and the questions below. Then listen to the passage on Henry Ford and answer the questions.

invent	self-taught mechanic	afford
mass production	Model T Ford	wages
stubborn	stylish	regain

1. Did Henry Ford invent the automobile?
2. What kind of education did Ford have?
3. Ford had two important ideas that led to the success of the Model T. What were they?
4. Many Americans viewed Ford as a folk hero. Why?
5. Why did Ford Motor Company lose its position as the leading car manufacturer? Can you think of other U.S. industries that have lost their positions of leadership?

Homework

1. Record the words and phrases in Practices 1 and 4.

2. Record the passage on Henry Ford on pages 145–146. Pay attention to your pronunciation of final consonants.

Related Units ▶ 4, 5, 18, 24, 30, 33, 35

UNIT 18

WORD ENDINGS:
PAST TENSE

🎧 The regular past tense of verbs in English has three pronunciations: [t], [d], and [əd] or [ɪd]. The pronunciation depends on the last sound in the base verb.

■ If the verb ends in a [t] or [d] sound, pronounce the past tense [əd] or [ɪd]. Pronounce the ending as a separate syllable. Listen.

wait/waited   land/landed   decide/decided   visit/visited

■ If the verb ends in a voiceless consonant other than [t], pronounce the past tense as the consonant [t]. Do *not* pronounce the ending as a separate syllable. Listen.

drop/dropped   like/liked   laugh/laughed   kiss/kissed

finish/finished   watch/watched

■ If the verb ends in a voiced consonant other than [d] or in a vowel, pronounce the past tense as the consonant [d]. Do *not* pronounce the ending as a separate syllable. Listen.

rob/robbed   breathe/breathed   love/loved   listen/listened

enter/entered   stay/stayed

Practice

🎧 **1. HEARING SYLLABLES.** Listen to the present and past verbs and underline the syllables. Write the number of syllables in the blanks. Then choose five pairs and say them out loud.

1. a. repeat _2_   3. a. investigate ___   5. a. create ___   7. a. expect ___
   b. repeated ___   b. investigated ___   b. created ___   b. expected ___

2. a. decide ___   4. a. end ___   6. a. paint ___   8. a. add ___
   b. decided ___   b. ended ___   b. painted ___   b. added ___

All of the present verbs in Practice 1 end in a _____ or _____ sound. The past tense ending in these verbs is pronounced as a new _____ .

2. HEARING ENDINGS. Listen to the present and past verbs and write the symbols for the bold-faced letters in the blanks. Then choose five pairs and say them out loud.

1. a. sto**p** [p]
   b. sto**pp**ed ___

2. a. ca**ll** ___
   b. ca**ll**ed ___

3. a. rea**ch** ___
   b. rea**ch**ed ___

4. a. hu**g** ___
   b. hu**gg**ed ___

5. a. a**sk** ___
   b. a**sk**ed ___

6. a. belie**ve** ___
   b. belie**ve**d ___

7. a. drea**m** ___
   b. drea**m**ed ___

8. a. contin**ue** ___
   b. contin**ue**d ___

None of the present verbs in Practice 2 ends in [t] or [d]. Therefore, the past tense ending (is/is not) pronounced as an extra syllable.

3. APPLYING THE RULE. Listen to the present verbs and use the rule to decide whether the past tense should be pronounced as an extra syllable. Write *yes* if the past tense ending is pronounced as an extra syllable and *no* if it is not. Then say the present and the past of each verb.

1. want _____

2. enjoy _____

3. vote _____

4. wash _____

5. demand _____

6. help _____

7. study _____

8. clean _____

4. THE PAST TENSE GAME. Play in two groups, A and B. Group A will read present verbs and Group B will give the past tense of the verbs. Then Group B will read their present verbs and Group A will give the past tense. Points are given for correct answers. (Group A's verbs are on page 150; Group B's verbs are on page 153.)

Example: A: *call*

B: *called*

S **5. JOINING.** Listen and repeat the phrases. Mark joinings. Then choose four phrases and say them out loud.

1. played_a game
2. watched it
3. started over
4. changed a lot

5. asked a question
6. cleaned it
7. handed it in
8. looked it up

6. DIALOGUES. Listen to the dialogues. Mark joinings and thought groups. Then practice reading the dialogues with a partner.

1. A: Are you ready for the test?

   B: I hope so. I studied_a lot last night.

2. A: Do you like American food?

   B: I hated it at first, but now I'm used to* it.

3. A: Why are you so late? What happened?

   B: I waited a long time for the bus, but it never came.

4. A: Did you find a new apartment last weekend?

   B: No. I looked at three apartments, but they were all too expensive.

*Pronounce *used to* as one word: [yuwstuw].

7. MEANING DIFFERENCES. Listen to the sentences. If you hear a past verb, write "So did I." If you hear a present verb, write "So do I."

1. I (need/needed) some money.   So _____ I.

2. I (travel/traveled) a lot.   So _____ I.

3. They (work/worked) hard.   So _____ I.

4. I (ask/asked) a lot of questions.   So _____ I.

5. They (watch/watched) the news.   So _____ I.

8. QUESTIONS AND ANSWERS. Write *Why* questions using the words below. Use past tense verbs in your answers. Then practice your dialogues with a partner, speaking as smoothly and clearly as you can.

> *Example:* *so happy?*
>
> Why are you so happy?
>
> I asked my boss for a raise and he agreed!

1. so tired?

   _____

   _____

   _____

2. so late?

   _____

   _____

   _____

3. so excited?

   _____

   _____

   _____

Homework

1. Read the words and phrases in Practices 1, 2, and 5.

2. Think of something that happened in the past that made you very happy. Record a short description of what happened, using the past tense.

Related Units ▶ 4, 5, 17, 30

UNIT 19

VOICED AND VOICELESS "th"

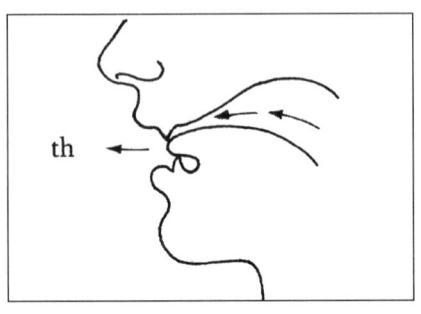

■ "Theta" [θ] is the beginning sound in *thing*, *thanks*, and *three*. It is a voiceless sound.

■ "Ethe" [ð] is the beginning sound in *this*, *those*, and *that*. It is a voiced sound.

Both sounds are made by placing the tip of the tongue between the teeth.

The correct pronunciation of theta and ethe is an important marker of an educated speaker of English.

Spelling and other details

▶ [θ] and [ð] are spelled *th*.

▶ Pronounce the *th* in *cloth*, but do not pronounce the *th* in *clothes*. *Clothes* is pronounced like the verb *close*.

▶ Pronounce the *th* of *Thai*, *Thailand*, and *Thames* as [t].

▶ Final [θ] or [ð] may be simplified or deleted in some words when an *-s* ending is added:

one month [θ]—two months [ts]

one-fifth[θ]—two-fifths [fs]

Practice

1. LISTEN AND PRACTICE. Listen and repeat the words with theta [θ]. Then choose five and say them out loud.

1. thing	5. three	9. author	13. fifth
2. think	6. thousand	10. nothing	14. bath
3. thanks	7. something	11. tooth	15. death
4. theater	8. healthy	12. mouth	16. south

2. LISTEN AND PRACTICE.   Listen and repeat the words with ethe [ð]. Then choose five and say them out loud.

1. this	5. these	9. mother	13. rather
2. that	6. then	10. weather	14. bathe
3. those	7. together	11. father	15. smooth
4. their	8. other	12. bother	16. breathe

3. LISTEN AND PRACTICE.   Listen and repeat the phrases. Then choose five and say them out loud.

1. thank you	5. thanks a lot	9. I think so.
2. a third	6. the fourth	10. I don't think so.
3. a thousand	7. over there	11. something else
4. I'd rather not.	8. this one	12. both of these

4. HEARING DIFFERENCES.   Listen and repeat the pairs of words. Listen again and circle the word you hear. Then choose three pairs and say them out loud.

1. a. math	3. a. thin	5. a. then	7. a. three
b. mass	b. tin	b. Zen	b. tree
2. a. with	4. a. breathe	6. a. thanks	8. a. thing
b. wit	b. breeze	b. tanks	b. sing

5. THE "th" GAME.   Play in two groups, A and B. Group A will ask questions and Group B will answer. Then Group B will ask Group A questions. All of the questions can be answered with a word or phrase containing a "th" sound. When answering a question, use appropriate intonation to show whether you are sure of the answer or unsure. If you are sure about the answer, use falling intonation. Use rising intonation to show you are unsure. (Group A's questions are on page 150; Group B's questions are on page 153.) Listen to the example.

Example: A: *What's 30 + 3?*

B: ___Thirty-three.___

A: *What's 378 × 63?*

B: ___About eighteen thousand?___

6. SENTENCES. Listen and repeat the sentences. Then choose a sentence and say it out loud. Speak slowly.

1. The third Thursday of November is Thanksgiving.
2. A "thingamajig" is something whose real name you can't think of.
3. Three hundred thirty-three thousand therapists thought about the new theory of thinking.
4. The seedy thieves threatened three dozen Southern mothers.

7. SPEAKING. In the United States, some birthdays are more important than others. Talk about why you think these birthdays are important, using the sentence:

I think (the first birthday) is important because . . .

1. the thirteenth birthday
2. the sixteenth birthday
3. the eighteenth birthday
4. the twentieth birthday
5. the twenty-first birthday
6. the thirtieth birthday
7. the fortieth birthday
8. the fiftieth birthday
9. the seventieth birthday

Which birthdays are special in your country?

Homework

1. Record the words, phrases, and sentences in Practices 1, 2, 3, and 6.

2. Choose two birthdays that you think are special and talk about them. Use Practice 7 as a model.

Related Units ▶ 4, 17, 29, 30

UNIT  20

THE CONSONANTS
[p, b, f, v, w]

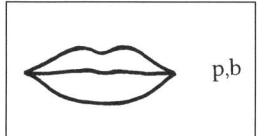

■ [p] is the sound in *pine* and [b] is the sound in *combine*. Both of these sounds are made by closing the lips. [p] is a voiceless sound and [b] is a voiced sound.

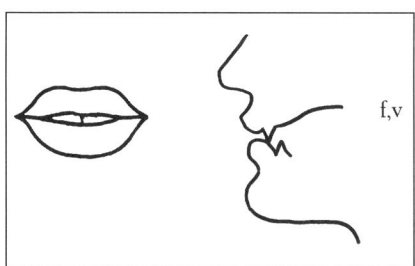

■ [f] is the sound in *fine* and [v] is the sound in *vine*. These sounds are made by gently touching your top teeth against the inside of your lower lip. The bottom lip protrudes a little. [f] is a voiceless sound and [v] is a voiced sound.

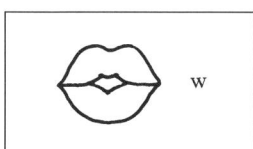

■ [w] is the sound in *wine*. [w] is made by rounding the lips. At the beginning of a word, the lips start very rounded and then unround. At the end of a word, the lips start unrounded and then round.

Spelling and other details

▶ [p, b, f, v, w] are usually spelled with the letters *p, b, f, v,* and *w.*

Other spellings

▶ [f]

　ph: al**ph**abet, tele**ph**one, **ph**otograph

　gh: enou**gh**, lau**gh**, tou**gh**, cou**gh**, rou**gh**

▶ [w]

　u: q**u**estion, sq**u**are, lang**u**age, q**u**iet, pers**u**ade

　wh (informal): **wh**ere, **wh**en, **wh**y, **wh**ile, **wh**ite

　once, one start with an unwritten [w].

▶ Silent letters

Silent p: *p̸sychology, p̸sychiatrist, receip̸t, coup̸, cup̸board, rasp̸berry*

Silent b: *thum̸b, bom̸b, com̸b, clim̸b, lam̸b, dou̸bt, de̸bt*

Silent w: *answ̸er, w̸rite, w̸rong, w̸rap, w̸rinkle, w̸reath, w̸hole, w̸ho*

Practice

1. LISTEN AND PRACTICE. Listen and repeat the words with [p]. Then choose four and say them out loud.

1. person
2. pink
3. copy
4. happy
5. cup
6. stop
7. people
8. population

2. LISTEN AND PRACTICE. Listen and repeat the words with [b]. Then choose four and say them out loud.

1. best
2. begin
3. lobby
4. about
5. rob
6. somebody
7. Bobby
8. baby

3. LISTEN AND PRACTICE. Listen and repeat the words with [f]. Then choose four and say them out loud.

1. fix
2. finish
3. awful
4. difficult
5. laugh
6. belief
7. fulfill
8. falafel

4. LISTEN AND PRACTICE. Listen and repeat the words with [v]. Then choose four and say them out loud.

1. very
2. voice
3. never
4. heaven
5. give
6. have
7. vivacious
8. convivial

5. LISTEN AND PRACTICE. Listen and repeat the words with [w]. Then choose four and say them out loud.

1. wind
2. want
3. language
4. away
5. beware
6. quietly
7. how
8. now
9. quiet
10. twenty
11. question
12. awake

6. HEARING DIFFERENCES. Listen and repeat the sets of words. Listen again and circle the word you hear. Then choose three sets and say them out loud.

1. a. berry
   b. very
   c. wary

2. a. pine
   b. fine
   c. wine

3. a. bull
   b. full
   c. wool

4. a. pest
   b. vest
   c. west

5. a. pear
   b. fair
   c. wear

6. a. Pow!
   b. vow
   c. Wow!

7. MOUTH SHAPES. Choose one of the word sets from Practice 6 and tell the class which set you have chosen. Face the class and mouth ("speak without sound") one of the words in the set you have chosen. The class will decide which word you "said" by the shape of your mouth. Look at the mouth diagrams on page 71 to help you.

8. LISTEN AND PRACTICE. Listen and repeat the phrases. Then choose four and say them out loud.

1. funny **people**
2. frozen **potatoes**
3. **wasteful** visitors
4. **tw**enty **qu**estions
5. voting **booth**
6. **wonderful poetry**
7. **purple** fingernails
8. foreign lan**gu**age
9. finger **pupp**ets
10. difficult **voca**bulary
11. **brave fire fighters**
12. **five** and a **quarter**

9. MEANING DIFFERENCES. Listen and repeat the words. Make sure you understand the words. Then work in pairs. Take turns asking for definitions. Pronounce the word carefully so your partner knows which word to define. Look at the example.

Example: A: *Look at the second pair. What does* _____"full"_____ *mean?*

 B: ___"Full" means "not empty."___

1. a. safe
   b. save

2. a. pull
   b. full

3. a. rope
   b. robe

4. a. Pete
   b. fcct

5. a. pig
   b. big

6. a. V
   b. we

7. a. vest
   b. best

8. a. pour
   b. bore

9. a. proof
   b. prove

10. THE [p, b, f, v, w] GAME.
Play in two groups, A and B. Group A will ask questions and Group B will answer. Then Group B will ask Group A questions. All of the questions can be answered with common words with [p], [b], [f], [v], or [w]. If a student answers with the correct word and pronounces it correctly, his or her group scores a point. (Group A's questions are on page 150; Group B's questions are on page 153.)

Example: A: __What's the opposite of an answer__ ?

B: __A question__ .

11. WORD SETS.
Choose two word sets and write sentences. You can change the order of the words and add other words. Underline thought groups so you can read the sentences smoothly. Practice your sentences with a partner and then read them out loud. Be sure to pronounce the bold-faced letters correctly.

Example: *please, copy, first, five, pages, book*

   __Please copy the first five pages of this book.__

1. gloves, frigid, **w**eather, frozen, fingers

_____

2. difficult, remember, voca**b**ulary, foreign, lang**u**age

_____

3. volley**b**all, **p**opular, s**p**ort, fun, **p**lay

_____

4. Picasso, famous, **p**ainter, **b**orn, Spain

_____

5. experts, **b**elieve, violence, television, **p**rograms, harmful, children

_____

6. box, **w**alnuts, **w**eigh, fifty-five, **p**ounds

_____

Homework

1. Record the words and phrases in Practices 1, 2, 3, 4, 5, 6, and 8.

2. Write sentences for all of the word sets in Practice 11 and record the sentences.

Related Units ▶ 4, 17, 29, 30

UNIT 21

VOICELESS [s] AND VOICED [z]

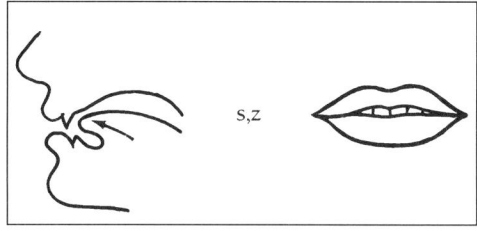

■ [s] occurs in *sister* and *nice*.

■ [z] is the sound in *rose* and *crazy*.

[s] and [z] are made with the tip of the tongue high, behind the top teeth. [s] is voiceless and [z] is voiced.

Some words that end in [s] as nouns or adjectives end in [z] as verbs. The vowel before the voiced [z] is longer than the vowel before voiceless [s].

NOUN/ADJECTIVE: [s]	VERB: [z]
a u**se**	to u**se**
an excu**se**	to excu**se**
the adv**ice**	to advi**se**
a cho**ice**	to choo**se**
a hou**se**	to hou**se**
a clo**se** relative	to clo**se** the door
a loo**se** shirt	to lo**se** something

Spelling and other details

▶ **[s]**

s: ye**s**, **s**ome, thi**s**, **s**i**s**ter

ss: me**ss**y, ki**ss**, cla**ss**, po**ss**ible

se: hor**se**, promi**se**, wor**se**, mou**se**

Other spellings

c (before *i, e, y*): **c**ent, **c**ity, **c**ircle, bi**c**ycle

ce: ni**ce**, poli**ce**, fen**ce**, offi**ce**

sc: **sc**ience, **sc**ent, **sc**enery, **sc**issors

x (pronounced [ks]): ne**x**t, e**x**cellent, e**x**ercise

In these words, *s* is silent: *i\$land, ai\$le.*

▶ **[z]**

z, zz, ze: **z**oo, cra**z**y, di**zz**y, si**ze**

s: ea**s**y, bu**s**y, mu**s**ic, vi**s**it

se: plea**se**, ri**se**, becau**se**, tho**se**

Other spellings

ss: **s**ci**ss**ors, de**ss**ert, po**ss**e**ss**

x (pronounced [gz]): e**x**ample, e**x**am, e**x**actly, e**x**istence

Practice

1. **VOICING.**   Place your fingers against the side of your throat. Make a long [zzzzzz] and feel the vibrations (the voicing). Now make a long [ssssss]; you will not feel any vibration during [ssssss] because [s] is voiceless.

   1. Alternate between [ssssss] and [zzzzzz] in the same breath. Feel the vibration (voicing) turn on and off.

   [ssssssszzzzzzzsssssszzzzzzzsssssszzzzzz]

   2. Alternate between [asssa] and [azzza]. Hold the [sss] and [zzz] as long as you can. Hear the difference.

2. **LISTEN AND PRACTICE.**   Listen and repeat the words with [z]. Then choose four and say them out loud. Lengthen the vowel before [z].

1. busy	5. buzz	9. was	13. easy
2. rose	6. raisin	10. cause	14. wise
3. dizzy	7. noise	11. reason	15. his
4. lazy	8. cousin	12. crazy	16. rising

3. **SOUNDS AND SPELLING.**   Listen and repeat the words. Write [z] or [s] to show the sound of the bold-faced letters. Then choose four and say them out loud.

1. choo**se** [z]	5. becau**se** ____	9. relea**se** ____
2. loo**se** ____	6. ro**se** ____	10. plea**se** ____
3. tho**se** ____	7. do**se** ____	11. sen**se** ____
4. noi**se** ____	8. cha**se** ____	12. accu**se** ____

4. **HEARING DIFFERENCES.**   Listen and repeat the pairs of words with [s] and [z]. Listen again and circle the word you hear. Then choose five pairs and say them out loud.

1. a. race	4. a. advice	7. a. racer	10. a. buses
b. raise	b. advise	b. razor	b. buzzes
2. a. lease	5. a. hiss	8. a. loose	11. a. noose
b. Lee's	b. his	b. lose	b. news
3. a. rice	6. a. place	9. a. lacy	12. a. Miss
b. rise	b. plays	b. lazy	b. Ms.

5. MEANING DIFFERENCES. Do this first with the class and then with a partner. Student A chooses the (a) or (b) phrase and says it out loud. Student B confirms what A said by asking, "Did you say, _____?," filling in the phrase B heard. B should use rising intonation with the question. If B heard correctly, A answers "Yes, I did." If B heard incorrectly, A answers "No, I said, _____." Listen to the examples.

Examples: A: ___He races cows___.

B: Did you say, ___"He raises cows"___?

A: No, I said, ___"He races cows"___.

A: ___He races cows___.

B: Did you say, ___"He races cows"___?

A: Yes, I did.

1. A. He races cows.   B. He raises cows.

2. A. Here's the racer.   B. Here's the razor.

3. A. The bus is too loud.   B. The buzz is too loud.

4. A. I like Miss Evans.   B. I like Ms. Evans.

5. A. He likes the place.   B. He likes the plays.

6. A. It's a great price.   B. It's a great prize.

Homework

1. Record the words in Practices 3 and 4.

2. Complete these sentences and record them. Be careful to pronounce the [s] and [z] sounds correctly. Lengthen vowels before [z].

a. I like peas [z] because [z] _____.

b. I like peace [s] because [z] _____.

c. Do you like that lacy [s] _____?

d. Do you like that lazy [z] _____?

e. Ms. Buzzy [z] [z] gave the roses [z][z] _____.

f. I like to listen [s] to music [z] when _____.

Related Units ▶ 4, 5, 17, 24, 29, 30, 36

UNIT 22

VOICELESS [ʃ] AND VOICED [ʒ]

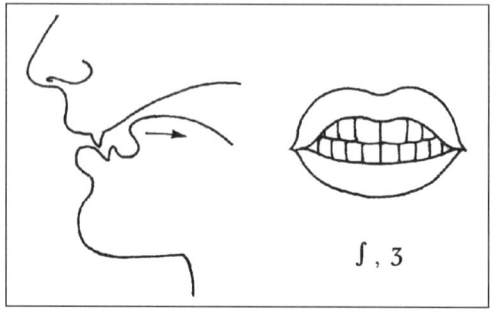

ʃ, ʒ

■ [ʃ] is the sound in *shoe, nation,* and *wash.*

■ [ʒ] is the sound in *television* and *beige.*

To make [ʃ] and [ʒ], the tongue is pulled back and up toward the roof of the mouth. The lips protrude slightly. [ʃ] is a voiceless sound and [ʒ] is a voiced sound.

Spelling and other details

▶ [ʃ]

  sh: **shop, wish, fashion**

Other spellings

  ti: **nation, condition, patient**

  ci: **special, musician, social**

  ssi: **permission, discussion, depression**

Unusual spellings

  machine, Chicago, chic, ocean, sure, sugar, insurance, pressure

▶ [ʒ]

  si: **decision, vision, television**

Other spellings

  su: **casual, treasure, pleasure, measure**

Practice

1. LISTEN AND PRACTICE.   Listen and repeat the words with [ʃ]. Then choose five and say them out loud.

1. **shoot**	6. **washer**	11. **cash**
2. **shine**	7. **national**	12. **shy**
3. **shoe**	8. **relation**	13. **wish**
4. **Chicago**	9. **vacation**	14. **push**
5. **sugar**	10. **pressure**	15. **finish**

2. LISTEN AND PRACTICE. Listen and repeat the words with [ʒ]. Then choose five and say them out loud.

1. decision
2. pleasure
3. Asia
4. division
5. usual
6. azure
7. measure
8. beige
9. leisure
10. television
11. explosion
12. vision

3. SOUNDS AND SPELLING. Listen to the words and decide if the sound of the bold-faced letters is [s], [ʃ], [z], or [ʒ]. Then write the word in the correct column.

1. super
2. sure
3. casual
4. result
5. visit
6. vision
7. promising
8. easier
9. expansion
10. racial
11. exercise
12. museum
13. massage
14. ocean
15. nice
16. pleasure

[s]	[ʃ]	[z]	[ʒ]
1. super			

Homework

1. Record the words in Practices 1 and 2.

2. Make a short recording describing a vacation. Use some of these words in your description (you don't need to use them all).

Michigan	vacation	fishing	ocean	treasure hunting
television	shows	relaxation	cruise ship	shore

Related Units ▶ 4, 17, 21, 24, 29, 30

UNIT 23

VOICELESS [tʃ] AND VOICED [dʒ]

■ [tʃ] is the sound in *chicken, watch,* and *richest.*

■ [dʒ] is the sound in *juice, age,* and *region.*

■ [tʃ] is a voiceless sound and [dʒ] is a voiced sound.

When [tʃ] or [dʒ] occurs at the end of a word and the following word begins with a consonant, pronounce the [tʃ] or [dʒ], but let it "die away" quickly. Do not release it strongly or put a little vowel sound between the two words. Then say the next word.

> watch' television   rich' woman   orange' color   language' teacher

When [tʃ] or [dʒ] occurs at the end a word and the following word begins with a vowel, join the final [tʃ] or [dʒ] to the vowel.

> catch a ball   lunch is over   college education   large enough

Sometimes students confuse [tʃ] and [ʃ] (*much* and *mush*) or [dʒ] and [ʒ] (*legion* and *lesion*). The difference between [tʃ] and [ʃ] is that [tʃ] starts with a [t] sound (the difference between [dʒ] and [ʒ] is that [dʒ] starts with a [d] sound). Be sure to pronounce the [t] of [tʃ] (even though you will not hear it as a separate sound). The [t] of [tʃ] makes words like *much* sound different from words like *mush* (likewise, be sure to pronounce the *d* of [dʒ]).

[tʃ]	[ʃ]	[dʒ]	[ʒ]
much	mush	legion	lesion
watch	wash	a Cajun	occasion

Spelling and other details

▶ [tʃ]

ch: lunch, chair, chance

(In a few words the letters *ch* have a [k] sound: *ache, chorus, Christmas;* in some words, the letters *ch* have a [ʃ] sound: *chef, Chicago, machine.*)

tch: watch, match, kitchen

Other spellings

t: picture, mixture, future, natural, question

c: cello, cellist

▶ [dʒ]

j: jazz, just, July

ge: George, dangerous, college

dge: bridge, edge, judge

Other spellings

du: graduate, education, individual

di: soldier

Practice

1. LISTEN AND PRACTICE.   Listen and repeat the words with [tʃ] and [dʒ]. Then choose four with each sound and say them out loud.

	[tʃ]		[dʒ]	
1. check	5. nature	9. jazz	13. pigeon
2. chalk	6. teacher	10. join	14. engine
3. cheap	7. catch	11. gym	15. age
4. kitchen	8. such	12. refrigerator	16. college

2. HEARING DIFFERENCES.   Listen and repeat the pairs of words in the sets below. Listen again and circle the word you hear. Then choose four pairs and say them out loud.

1. a. choice
   b. Joyce

2. a. edge
   b. etch

3. a. occasion
   b. a Cajun

4. a. mush
   b. much

5. a. legion
   b. lesion

6. a. H
   b. age

7. a. cheap
   b. sheep

8. a. cash
   b. catch

9. a. pledger
   b. pleasure

(S) 3. LISTEN AND PRACTICE. Listen and repeat the phrases. Then choose two from each column and say them out loud. In Column A, pronounce the final [tʃ] or [dʒ] but do not release it strongly. In Column B, join the final [tʃ] or [dʒ] smoothly to the vowel.

A	B
1. match' book	7. charge‿a shirt
2. orange' drink	8. watch‿a show
3. strange' noise	9. exchange‿addresses
4. age' limit	10. such‿a good time
5. how much' money	11. large‿apartment
6. which' one	12. teach‿English

Now choose a phrase from each column and make a sentence for each phrase. Read your sentence out loud.

4. INTERVIEWS. First listen and repeat the occupations below. Then ask a classmate a question about each occupation.

Example: A: What's _a soldier_ ? B: _A soldier is someone who's in the army_ .

1. a. a soldier	3. a. a judge	5. a. a butcher
b. a jazz musician	b. a teacher	b. a forest ranger
2. a. a matchmaker	4. a. an engineer	6. a. a travel agent
b. a store manager	b. a fortune-teller	b. a cellist

Now imagine that you have to choose one of the two occupations in the sets above. Interview a classmate and report your partner's preferences to the class.

Homework

1. Record the words and phrases in Practices 1, 2, and 3.

2. Choose two occupations from Practice 4—one that you would like to have and one that you would not like to have. Describe what is done in each profession and explain why you would (would not) like to have that occupation. Speak as smoothly and clearly as you can.

Related Units ▶ 4, 17, 22, 30

UNIT 24

WORD ENDINGS: PLURALS AND PRESENT TENSE

The -s ending of plural nouns and third person singular present verbs has three pronunciations: [s], [z], and [əz] or [ɪz]. The pronunciation depends on the last sound of the base verb or noun.

■ If the noun or verb ends in a sibilant sound, [s], [z], [ʃ], [ʒ], [tʃ], [dʒ], or an *x* (which sounds like [ks]), pronounce the ending as an extra syllable, [əz] or [ɪz].

one boss   two bosses   one judge   two judges

I rise   He rises   I fix   He fixes

■ If the noun or verb ends in the voiceless sound [p], [t], or [k], pronounce the ending as [s]. Do not pronounce it as a new syllable.

one street   two streets   I hope   He hopes   I smoke   He smokes

■ If the noun or verb ends in a voiced sound [b], [d], [g], [v], [r], [l], [m], [n], [ŋ], or a vowel, pronounce the ending as [z]. Do not pronounce it as a new syllable.

one dog   two dogs   one head   two heads   one day   two days

I love   He loves   I rob   He robs   one car   two cars

■ Many nouns that end in [f] change [f] to [v] in the plural and add the ending [z]. If a verb ends in [f], pronounce the ending as [s].

Nouns: knife   knives   half   halves   leaf   leaves

Verbs: laugh   laughs   cough   coughs   goof   goofs

■ If a noun ends in [θ], pronounce the ending as [s]. The final [θ] may be simplified or deleted in the plural.

month   months [mǝnts]   fifth   fifths [fɪfs]

The plural word *clothes* is pronounced like the verb in *close the door.*

■ If a verb ends in [ð], pronounce the ending as [z]. Sometimes the [ð] may be deleted and the [z] ending is lengthened ("z̄" means "long z").

bathe   bathes [beyz̄]   breathe   breathes [briyz̄] or [briðz]

1. HEARING SYLLABLES. Listen and repeat the singular and plural noun pairs. Underline the syllables. Then choose four pairs and say them out loud. The plural ending is pronounced as a new syllable.

1. a. b<u>ox</u>
   b. b<u>ox</u><u>es</u>

2. a. catch
   b. catches

3. a. wish
   b. wishes

4. a. dress
   b. dresses

5. a. rose
   b. roses

6. a. choice
   b. choices

7. a. pass
   b. passes

8. a. kiss
   b. kisses

9. a. age
   b. ages

2. APPLYING THE RULE. Listen to the nouns. Write the last sound of the singular noun (the bold-faced letters) in the first blank. Write the plural noun in the second blank, and underline the syllables in both the singular and plural nouns. Write *yes* if the plural ending is pronounced as a new syllable and write *no* if it is not. Then choose three singular-plural pairs and say them out loud.

SOUND	PLURAL	NEW SYLLABLE?
1. bo<u>ok</u> _k_	<u>books</u>	no
2. ta**x** ____	_____	_____
3. smi**le** ____	_____	_____
4. sandwi**ch** ____	_____	_____
5. wind**ow** ____	_____	_____
6. pri**ze** ____	_____	_____
7. lea**f** ____	_____	_____
8. bu**s** ____	_____	_____
9. exerci**se** ____	_____	_____
10. moth**er** ____	_____	_____
11. sta**te** ____	_____	_____
12. mon**th** ____	_____	_____

3. HEARING ENDINGS.

Work in pairs. Read a verb phrase to your partner. Make the verb either third person singular (add the ending) or third person plural (no ending). Your partner will make a sentence starting with *He/She* or *They*. Pronounce the verb carefully so your partner knows which subject to use. Then switch roles.

Example: play the guitar

A: plays the guitar

B: She plays the guitar.

1. answer the phone politely
2. close the windows
3. always miss the bus
4. eat only vegetables
5. write well
6. speak Chinese
7. walk to work
8. live near the park
9. lose things
10. worry a lot
11. fix computers
12. teach dancing
13. bathe in the morning
14. pass my house every day

4. U.S. GOVERNMENT AND VERB ENDINGS.

The Constitution of the United States divides the powers of government among the three branches of government: the executive branch (the president and his cabinet, or advisors); the legislative branch (Congress—the House of Representatives and the Senate); and the judicial branch (the courts). Work in pairs. Student A reads a verb phrase that describes the U.S. government. Make the verb third person singular or third person plural. Your partner will complete the sentence with the correct form of the subject. Pronounce the verb clearly so your classmate knows whether to use a singular or plural subject.

Example: A: lives in the White House

B: The president lives in the White House.

VERB PHRASE	SUBJECTS
1. live in the White House	the president/presidents
2. serve for two years	a representative/representatives
3. serve for six years	a senator/senators
4. serve for life	a Supreme Court justice/Supreme Court justices
5. make laws	Congress/the House and the Senate
6. appoint judges to the Supreme Court	the president/presidents
7. approve appointments to the Court	the Senate/senators

(continued on next page)

8. make treaties with other countries   the president/presidents

9. approve treaties made by the president   Congress/the House and Senate

10. serve as the head of the Senate   the vice president/vice presidents

11. vote only when the Senate is tied   the vice president/vice presidents

12. initiate legislation to spend money   the House/representatives

13. vote on this legislation   the Senate/senators

14. have the power to veto legislation passed by Congress   the president/presidents

15. serve as commander-in-chief of the armed forces   the president/presidents

16. appoint members of the cabinet   the president/presidents

Homework

1. Record the words in Practices 1 and 2.

2. Write down some information about the government in your country. Record the information. Pronounce plural noun and present tense verb endings carefully.

Related Units ▶ 4, 5, 17, 21 30

UNIT  25

CONSONANT CONTRASTS: [r] AND [l]

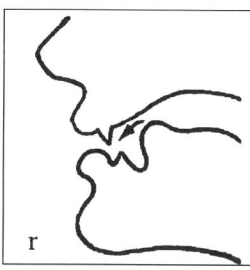

r

■ [r] is the sound in *red* and *road*.

To make [r], the tongue starts in a turned back position and then "uncurls." It does **not** touch the top of the mouth as it uncurls.

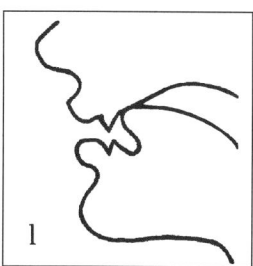

l

■ [l] is the sound in *like* and *left*.

To make [l], touch the tip of your tongue just behind the top teeth.

Spelling and other details

The letter *w* is silent before *r* : *w̶rite, w̶rong, w̶ring, w̶restle, w̶rap, w̶reck, w̶rist.*

The letter *l* is silent in these words: *wal̶k, tal̶k, chal̶k, hal̶f, cal̶f, woul̶d, coul̶d, shoul̶d, yol̶k.*

◢◢◢◢◢◢◢ Practice ◢◢◢◢◢◢◢

 1. LISTEN AND PRACTICE. Listen and repeat the words with [r]. Then choose five and say them out loud. Pronounce the words slowly.

1. red	5. rich	9. sorry
2. write	6. ready	10. crime
3. room	7. arrive	11. try
4. repeat	8. correct	12. crowd

Listen and repeat the words with [l]. Then choose five and say them out loud. Pronounce the words slowly.

1. left	5. like	9. collect
2. long	6. listen	10. climb
3. last	7. a lot	11. fly
4. love	8. alive	12. cloud

(S) **3. HEARING DIFFERENCES.** Listen and repeat the pairs of words with [r] and [l]. Listen again and circle the word you hear. Then choose three pairs and say them out loud.

1. a. lay	3. a. arrive	5. a. glass	7. a. Ellie
b. Ray	b. alive	b. grass	b. airy
2. a. weary	4. a. list	6. a. climb	8. a. right
b. Willy	b. wrist	b. crime	b. light

4. MEANING DIFFERENCES. Look at the road map of the town of Logan. Listen and repeat the sentences below.

1. Logan Road is the main road in the town of Logan.

2. Logan Road runs north and south.

3. Rocket Road and Locket Road run east and west.

4. Glassy Lane and Grassy Lane run north and south.

5. Myla's Drive and Myra's Drive also run north and south.

6. There are twelve businesses on Glassy Lane, Grassy Lane, Myla's Drive, and Myra's Drive.

Roy's Restaurant   Mary's Clothing Store   Logan Medical Clinic   Larry's Florist Shop

Locket Road

Grassy Lane   Ellie's Beauty Salon   Glassy Lane   Milly's Art Gallery   Logan Road   Myra's Drive   Logan Electric Company   Myla's Drive   Myla's Restaurant

Rocket Road

Logan Library   Laura's Stationery Store   Gary's Garage   Roland's Shoe Repair

Start

Work in pairs. Choose one of the twelve places on Glassy Lane, Grassy Lane, Myla's Drive, or Myra's Drive, but don't tell your partner the name of the place. Give your partner two directions to get to the place you chose. Then ask your partner where he or she is. Pronounce the [r] or [l] of the street names carefully so your partner knows which street to turn on.

Example: A: *Go north on Logan Road. Turn* __right__ *on* __Locket Road__.
right/left   road name

Then turn __left__ *on* __Myla's Drive__.
right/left   road name

Where are you?

B: *I'm at* __Larry's Florist Shop__.
business name

5. SPEAKING.   Work in groups of four or five and list as many countries as you can that have [r] or [l] in their names. Then choose a country that you would like to visit and tell the class why. Try to include some of the [r] and [l] words below, and speak as smoothly and clearly as you can.

I'd like to go/travel	interesting place(s)	beautiful scenery
river	lake	coastline
island(s)	history, historical	friendly

Europe	Middle East	Asia	Latin America	Africa
France	Lebanon	Korea	Colombia	Morocco
_____	_____	_____	_____	_____
_____	_____	_____	_____	_____
_____	_____	_____	_____	_____

Homework

1. Record the words in Practices 1, 2, and 3.

2. Give directions to the places below using the map in Practice 4.

   Roy's Restaurant

   Example: *First, drive on Logan Road. Turn* __left__ *on* __Locket Road__.

   Then turn __right__ *on* __Grassy Lane__. *You'll see*

   __Roy's Restaurant__ *on your* __left__.

   a. Myla's Restaurant   c. Gary's Garage
   b. Laura's Stationery Store   d. Logan Medical Clinic

Related Units ▶ 4, 13, 29, 30

U N I T  26

NASAL CONSONANTS: [m], [n], AND [ŋ]

- [m], [n], and [ŋ] are called nasal sounds. The air comes out the nose.

- [m] is the sound in *mouth, summer,* and *home.* [m] is made by closing the lips and letting the air pass out through the nose.

- [n] is the sound in *nose, snake,* and *nine.* [n] is made by touching the tongue tip behind the top teeth and letting the air pass out through the nose.

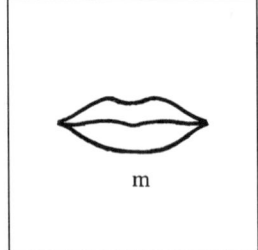
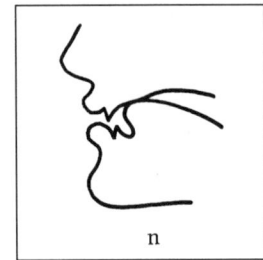
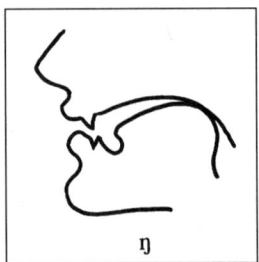

- [ŋ] is the sound in *singer, hang,* and *long.* [ŋ] is made by touching the back of the tongue against the back top of the mouth and letting the air pass out through the nose. [ŋ] can occur in the middle of a word or at the end of a word, but it never begins a word in English. *-ng* is the common spelling of [ŋ]. In many *-ng* spellings, the [g] is not pronounced (for example, *sing* does not have a [g] sound). In a few words, like *finger,* the [g] is pronounced. In addition, several adjectives that end in [ŋ] add a [g] sound in the comparative and superlative.

ADJECTIVE (NO [g])	COMPARATIVE AND SUPERLATIVE ([g])
young athlete [ŋ]	younger, youngest [ŋg]
long ago [ŋ]	longer, longest [ŋg]
strong engine [ŋ]	stronger, strongest [ŋg]

When nasal consonants end words, be sure to pronounce them strongly and distinctly as consonants. In some languages, final nasals "nasalize" a preceding vowel and can be dropped; for example, a word like *ham* might be pronounced as *hã* (~ shows that the vowel has been nasalized). Do not drop final nasals in English. They must be heard distinctly as consonants. Join final nasal consonants to following vowels.

hum a song run away sing alto

Spelling and other details

▶ [m]

 m, mm: **mom, May, summer, small**

Other spellings

 mn (silent *n*): **autumn, hymn**

▶ [n]

 n, nn: **none, never, snake, sunny**

Other spellings

 kn, gn: **know, knee, knife, foreign, sign**

▶ [ŋ]

 ng: **sing, ringing, wrong, young**

 n before g, k: **English, angry, bank, think**

/////////////// Practice ///////////////

1. LISTEN AND PRACTICE. Listen and repeat the words. Then choose three from each column and say them out loud.

[m]	[n]	[ŋ]	[ŋg, ŋk]
1. most	7. nail	13. sing	19. drink
2. messy	8. necessary	14. wrong	20. thank
3. important	9. friendly	15. ring	21. bank
4. stomach	10. happen	16. hanging	22. anger
5. some	11. poison	17. ping-pong	23. longer
6. home	12. done	18. young	24. younger

2. HEARING ENDINGS. Listen and repeat the words. Write *yes* in the blank after the word if you hear a [g] or [k] sound. Write *no* if you do not.

1. fang *no*

2. longer _____

3. winging _____

4. strongest _____

5. a strong army _____

6. thank you _____

7. linger _____

8. gang _____

9. clanging _____

3. BINGO. Listen to each word and write the consonant symbol [m], [n], or [ŋ] below it. Repeat the words. Then listen again and cross out each word you hear. When you have a complete row or column crossed out, shout out "Bingo!"

1. ring [ŋ]	6. Tim	11. Jan	16. sinner
2. hang	7. sung	12. king	17. simmer
3. kin	8. jam	13. singer	18. sun
4. bang	9. Kim	14. some	19. Bam!
5. rim	10. ban	15. tin	20. ham

4. EXPANDING VOICE RANGE. Work in pairs to complete the dialogues. Use the words in parentheses to respond to all of the questions in a set. Draw the intonation patterns. Use strong intonation to show strong feelings. Pronounce the bold-faced consonants correctly. Practice the dialogues with your partner. Listen to the example.

Example: (a long time)

a. A: *You look so young and refreshed today! How long did you sleep last night?*

   B: ___A long time___ .

b. A: *How long does it take to drive from Toronto to New York?*

   B: *I don't know.* ___A long time___ ?

c. A: *I think there may be something wrong with my eyes. It takes me a really long time to blink.*

   B: *To blink?* ___A long time___ ??

1. (**no one**)

   a. A: You **kno**w, I we**nt** to the cockpit of this pla**ne** and **no one** is there!

       B: _____ ???!!!!

   b. A: Who just called?

       B: _____ . The phone's not working.

   c. A: Here's a trivia question for you. How **many** people in this city are over 125 years old?

       B: I don't **kno**w. _____ ?

2. (an opera si**ng**er)

   a. A: A famous opera si**ng**er put the **new** roof **on my** house.

       B: _____ ????????!!!!!!!!!!!!!!!!

   b. A: She's taki**ng** voice lessons. Does she want to be a si**ng**er?

       B: Yes, _____ .

   c. A: His **mo**ther used to si**ng** professionally. Do you **kno**w what she was?

       B: I'**m no**t sure. _____ ?

5. INTERVIEWS. Work in groups of four or five and find the answers to these questions. Then report them to the class. Speak slowly and clearly and pronounce the nasal consonants correctly.

   1. Who can hold his or her breath the longest?
   2. Who is the strongest (who can lift the heaviest weight)?
   3. Who has been in this city the longest?
   4. Who is the hungriest at breakfast time?
   5. Who has the longest index finger?
   6. Who likes to sing the most? (Who sings the best?)
   7. Who has the youngest sibling?

Homework

1. Record the words in Practices 1 and 2.

2. Write sentences using all of the words in the sets below and record them.
   a. king, ring, thank, banker
   b. youngest, one, compete, ping-pong tournament
   c. drink, stomach, hangover
   d. single, winner, contest, European, vacation

Related Units ▶ 4, 5, 17, 29, 30

UNIT

CONSONANT CONTRASTS:
[y] AND [dʒ];
CONSONANT CLUSTERS
WITH [y]

■ [y] is the beginning sound in *yes, you,* and *union.*

When you make [y], the center of the tongue slides up toward the front of the mouth.

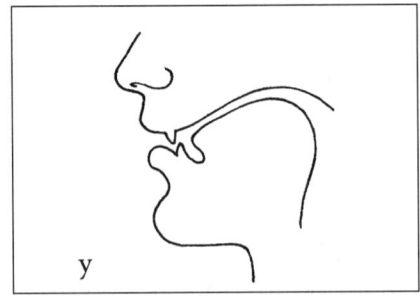

■ [y] is the second sound in several consonant clusters (consonant groups). The [y] sound may be hard to recognize because the letter *y* is usually not written.

      re**gu**lar [gy]   parti**cu**lar [ky]   voca**bu**lary [by]   po**pu**lar [py]

■ [y] is also the last sound of several vowels. It is the last sound of the diphthongs [ay] and [oy]: *my* [may] and *boy* [boy]. It is also the last sound of the vowels [iy] and [ey]: *see* [siy] and *say* [sey]. When these vowels are followed by another vowel, join [y] to the next vowel.

      my‿uncle   enjoy‿it   see‿it   say‿it

If your native language is Spanish, you may pronounce [y] too much like [dʒ], so that *yet* and *jet* sound the same. If this is a problem, do not let your tongue make firm contact with the top of your mouth when you say [y] words (the contact produces the [dʒ] sound). Instead, start [y] words with a long vowel: iiiiiiies *(yes).*

Spelling and other details

▶ [y]

y: **yellow**, **yard**, **yawn**, be**yond**

u (after [p, b, m, f, k, g, h]): po**pu**lar, am**bu**lance, **mu**sic, **fu**ture, ex**cu**se, ar**gue**, **hu**mor

u (at the beginning of a word, but not in the prefix *un-*): **use**, **un**ion

u (after *n* and *l* if *u* is unstressed): **Ja**nuary, **val**ue, **vol**ume

i (after *n* and *l* if *i* is unstressed): **on**ion, con**ven**ient, fa**mil**iar, **mill**ion

ew, iew (pronounced [yuw]): **few**, **view**

eau (pronounced [yuw]): **beau**tiful

Practice

1. LISTEN AND PRACTICE. Listen and repeat the words with [y]. Then choose five and say them out loud.

1. year
2. united
3. yell
4. yeast
5. yard
6. beyond
7. yet
8. usual
9. yesterday
10. young
11. yield
12. university
13. useful
14. yolk
15. yogurt
16. youth

2. LISTEN AND PRACTICE. Listen and repeat the words with [y] clusters. Then choose four and say them out loud.

1. com**pu**ter
2. **Hou**ston
3. inter**view**
4. o**pin**ion
5. **mu**sic
6. par**ti**cular
7. pe**cu**liar
8. po**pu**lation
9. vo**ca**bulary
10. **beau**tiful
11. **re**gular
12. **fi**gure

3. SENTENCES. Listen and repeat the sentences with [y] and [dʒ]. Mark thought groups and joinings. Then choose three and say them out loud.

1. You can't go to Yale if you're in jail.
2. Usually yellow jello has a banana flavor.
3. Yes, Jess made John yawn.
4. Yesterday, the Jester told such a good joke about egg yolks that the king yelped with laughter.
5. His successful use of young jungle animals made his film this year a hit, but he's not rich enough to buy a jet yet.
6. If you go to the store, I could use some juice, some yams, some jam, and some yeast.

4. IDIOMS AND EXPRESSIONS.

Listen and repeat the idioms with [y] clusters in Column A. Write a small *y* where it is pronounced. Match the idioms to the definitions in Column B. Then choose an idiom and ask a classmate to define it, using a complete sentence.

A	B
1. the partic^yulars	a. elderly people
2. a regular guy	b. the details
3. figure it out	c. to be found only in that place
4. one chance in a million	d. a nice normal person
5. senior citizens	e. a very small chance
6. a security blanket	f. know many words
7. puritan beliefs	g. discover the solution
8. have an extensive vocabulary	h. something that makes one feel safe
9. to be peculiar to a place	i. rigid beliefs that pleasure is wrong
10. few and far between	j. rare, uncommon, or unusual

5. DIALOGUES.

Listen and repeat the dialogues. Mark joinings. Write a small *y* where there are joinings of unwritten [y]s. Then practice reading the dialogues with a partner.

1. A: Do you want to see^ya movie tonight?

   B: Do I^yever!

2. A: This reading will take me hours and hours of time!

   B: No excuses! You promised to help me out!

3. A: How are you going to get there?

   B: I'll fly if I can afford it.

4. A: I'm afraid your answer is way off.

   B: Let me try it again.

Homework

1. Record the words in Practices 1 and 2.

2. Choose two dialogues from Practice 5 and record them. Then think of a situation in which each dialogue might take place and describe it (for example, what are the people in the dialogue talking about, where are they, what is their relationship, and so forth).

Related Units ▶ 3, 4, 5, 17, 23, 29, 30

UNIT 28

THE CONSONANT [h]

■ [h] is the sound in *hat, heavy,* and *ahead.*

[h] is made by pushing air out of the lungs. It is similar to the sound of hard breathing after exercise. When you make [h], the back of the tongue should not be close to the top of the mouth.

When unstressed pronouns and possessives (*he, him, his, her*) beginning with [h] are used inside a sentence, the [h] is usually dropped. If you drop the [h], you must join the pronoun or possessive to the preceding word. [h] is not dropped when the pronoun or possessive starts the sentence.

His parents gave ̶him a computer for ̶his birthday.
[h]

Spelling and other details

▶ [h]

  h: **h**ungry, **h**eart, **h**old, in**h**erit

Other spellings

  wh: **wh**o, **wh**ose, **wh**om, **wh**ole

[h] is never pronounced in these words: *h̶our, h̶onest, h̶onor, h̶eir, h̶erb, veh̶icle, exh̶aust, exh̶ibit.*

░░░░░ Practice ░░░░░

1. LISTEN AND PRACTICE. Listen and repeat the words with [h]. Then choose three and say them out loud.

1. happen	4. behind	7. overhear	10. inhale
2. healthy	5. home	8. harmful	11. ahoy
3. house	6. inhabit	9. hint	12. humor

🔊 **2. SOUNDS AND SPELLING.** Listen and repeat the words. Make a line through the letter *h* if it is not pronounced.

1. ~~h~~our
2. head
3. humid
4. herb
5. heavy
6. behind
7. honesty
8. inherit
9. unhappy
10. alcohol
11. honorable
12. behave
13. vehicle
14. hot
15. however
16. heir

🎧 **3. IDIOMS AND EXPRESSIONS.** Listen and repeat the idioms in Column A. Cross out silent *h*s and mark joinings. Match the idioms to the definitions in Column B. Then choose an idiom and ask a classmate to define it, using a complete sentence.

A	B
1. eleventh ~~h~~our	a. to refuse to face reality
2. to learn by heart	b. to gain an advantage
3. to hold still	c. the last possible moment to do something
4. to make an honest living	d. to be useful
5. in hot water	e. to memorize
6. a man of his word	f. someone who keeps his promises
7. heavy-handed	g. to stay motionless
8. not so hot	h. to cause trouble for someone
9. to come in handy	i. to search everywhere
10. to bury one's head in the sand	j. unable to be helped
11. honor-bound	k. clumsy; oppressive
12. to get the upper hand	l. not very good
13. to search high and low	m. in trouble
14. beyond help	n. required by one's honor to do something
15. to give someone a hard time	o. to earn one's pay fairly, without breaking any laws

4. MEANING DIFFERENCES. Work in pairs. Complete a sentence with one of the words in parentheses and read the sentence to your partner. Pronounce the word carefully so your partner knows which response to choose. If you choose a word that begins with a vowel, join it to the preceding word. Then switch roles.

Example: I (hate, ate) ice cream.

a. You'll never lose weight eating that!

(b.) Most people love it.

1. Do you use (air spray / hair spray)?
   a. No, it makes my hair sticky.
   b. No, I just open a window.

2. Did you hear that (howl/owl)?
   a. Yes, there must be coyotes around.
   b. Yes, it lives in the big tree beside the house.

3. The (heart/art) organization put out this booklet.
   a. It urges people to eat less fat and exercise regularly.
   b. It describes the new exhibit that will be opening at the museum.

4. Please (eat up/heat up) the chicken.
   a. I can't. I'm allergic to it.
   b. It's much better served cold.

Homework

1. Record the words in Practice 2.

2. Complete the sentences. Underline thought groups. Cross out silent *h*s and mark joinings. Then record the sentences.

   a. An ~~h~~onest man ___found the wallet and returned it___ .

   b. Eva and her brother _____ .

   c. In an hour _____ .

   d. If he goes, _____ .

   e. Where did his _____ ?

Related Units ▶ 4, 5, 6

UNIT  BEGINNING CONSONANT CLUSTERS

Many words in English begin with consonant clusters (groups of consonants). When you say these words, pronounce the consonants closely together. Do not separate them with a vowel sound.

CONSONANT CLUSTER	CONSONANT + VOWEL
prayed	**pa**rade
claps	**co**llapse
sport	**su**pport

■ Clusters with [s].

spot	**st**ay	**sc**ore	**sm**all	**sn**ake	**sw**ing
slow	**spr**ing	**spl**it	**str**ong	**scr**eam	

Native Spanish-speakers sometimes add a short [ɛ] sound before [s] clusters that begin English words. If this is a problem for you, practice [s] clusters by holding a long [sssss] and then pronouncing the rest of the word: *sssssstate*. If you add an [ɛ] sound to the beginning of an [s] cluster, you may say a word you do not intend.

state   **est**ate   **st**eam   **est**eem

■ Clusters with [r] and [l].

pray	**pl**ay	**br**eak	**bl**ue	**tr**ain	**dr**ive	**cr**y
climb	**gr**ow	**gl**ass	**thr**ee	**fr**ee	**fl**y	**sl**eep

■ Clusters with [w].

twelve   **dw**ell   **qu**ick   **Gw**en   **sw**ear

If your native language is Korean, you may not pronounce the [w] sound in words like *question* ([kwɛstʃən]) clearly enough. If this is a problem, round your lips as you make the [k] sound, and *unround* them as you pronounce the vowel (unrounding produces the [w] sound before a vowel).

■ Rare clusters. These clusters occur in only a few words.

[ʃr]	**shr**ink	**shr**ub	**shr**ivel
[sf]	**sph**ere		
[sr]	**sy**ringe		

Practice

1. LISTEN AND PRACTICE. Listen and repeat the words. Then choose two from each column and say them out loud.

1. **sm**ell	7. **gr**ay	13. **fl**ower	19. **qu**estion
2. **st**ay	8. **br**own	14. **gl**ad	20. **qu**iet
3. **sn**ow	9. **thr**ow	15. **fl**at	21. **qu**ick
4. **str**anger	10. **tr**ee	16. **cl**oudy	22. **tw**in
5. **spl**endid	11. **dr**aw	17. **pl**ant	23. **Gw**en
6. **sch**ool	12. **fr**ighten	18. **bl**ouse	24. **shr**ink

2. HEARING DIFFERENCES. Listen and repeat the pairs of words. Listen again and circle the word you hear. Then choose three pairs and say them out loud.

1. a. parade	3. a. polite	5. a. Clyde
b. prayed	b. plight	b. collide
2. a. esteem	4. a. state	6. a. estrange
b. steam	b. estate	b. strange

3. SENTENCES. Listen and repeat the sentences. Mark thought groups and joinings. Then choose two and say them out loud.

1. The estate taxes are higher than the state taxes.
2. We prayed the parade would proceed as planned.
3. Please ask the police where they got their splendid trousers.
4. There's brown glass on the green grass.
5. I scream, you scream, we all scream for ice cream.
6. Twelve twins twisted the ropes as they swung on Gwen's swing.
7. You were smart to order those snazzy, small snails.
8. Answer the quiz questions quickly but quietly, and don't forget to quote the queen.
9. The crowd of clever climbers clad in clean climbing clothes crossed the clearing to the cliff.

🎧 **4. EXPANDING VOICE RANGE.** Work in pairs to complete the dialogues. Use the words in parentheses to respond to all of the questions in a set. Draw the intonation patterns. Use strong intonation to show strong feelings. Pay attention to the bold-faced consonant clusters. Practice the dialogues with your partner. Listen to the example.

Example: (the **queen**)

a. A: The **queen** is the new heavyweight boxer of England.

   B: _____ The queen _____ ???!!!!

b. A: Arthur was the king. What was Guinevere, his wife?

   B: _____ The queen _____ .

c. A: Who is the most famous person in England?

   B: _____ The queen _____ ?

1. (**plastic flowers**)

   a. A: When I get married, I want to carry a nice bouquet of **plastic flowers**.

      B: _____ ????!!!!!!!!

   b. A: What kind of **flowers** aren't real?

      B: _____ .

   c. A: What do you think she has in her window?

      B: I don't know. _____ ?

2. (**French flies**)

   a. A: What kind of **flies** live in **France**?

      B: I don't know. _____ ?

   b. A: I had the most delicious **French flies** for dinner last night!

      B: _____ !!!???

   c. A: When you were in Europe, were you ever bitten by German **flies**?

      B: No. Only _____ .

3. (a complete **str**anger)

    a. A: What do you call someone you've never met?

        B: _____ ?

    b. A: Bad news. Dad's decided to give the family fortune to a com**p**lete **str**anger!

        B: _____ !!!!!????

    c. A: Do you know Raymond?

        B: No, he's _____ .

Homework

Record the words and sentences in Practices 1, 2, and 3.

Related Units ▶ 4, 17, 19, 20, 21, 22, 25, 26, 28, 30

UNIT 30

FINAL CONSONANT CLUSTERS

Many English words end in consonant clusters: *help, test, large, glimpse*. Grammatical endings like the past or present may create even bigger consonant clusters.

change [ndʒ]	changed [ndʒd]
like [k]	liked [kt]
dog [g]	dogs [gz]
shark [rk]	sharks [rks]

■ Final consonant clusters are often followed by words that also begin with consonant clusters. As a result, some very large groups of consonants can occur in English.

helped strangers
[lpt str]

■ Because English allows a greater number and combination of final consonants than many other languages, the pronunciation of the ends of words is sometimes difficult. In most words, you must pronounce all of the consonants in a final cluster and all of the consonants that follow that word. You should not separate consonants, and you should not simplify the clusters. Here are some strategies to help you pronounce final consonants.

• Identical consonants. When one word ends with a consonant and the next word begins with the same consonant, hold one long consonant. Do not say the same consonant twice.

grea͞t trip   dre͞ss simply   har͞d day   wor͞k quickly

• Different consonants. When a final consonant is followed by a different consonant, hold the final consonant until you're ready to say the next word. Do not release the final consonant or separate the words with a little vowel sound.

rob' diamonds	finished' quickly	sharp' knife
[b' d]	[ʃt' kw]	[rp' n]

- Consonant + vowel. When a word ends in a consonant and the next word begins with a vowel, join the consonant to the vowel.

  amazed‿audience   loves‿onions   answered‿a question

- Simplifications. Sometimes consonants in clusters are simplified by omitting them. This happens most often when the middle consonant is a voiceless stop ([p, t, k]). Often the final sound will be held longer to hold the "place" of the omitted middle consonant. Sounds representing grammatical endings are never omitted.

  gif~~t~~s   as~~k~~ed   ac~~t~~s
  [gɪfs̄]   [æst]   [æks̄]

- Final clusters with "th" sounds. [θ] is sometimes omitted when it is followed by another consonant. It is not omitted otherwise.

  one month   two mon~~th~~s
  [nθ]   [nts]

Practice

1. LISTEN AND PRACTICE.   Listen and repeat the phrases. Then choose four and say them out loud. Hold one long consonant where the words join.

1. red door	5. half full	9. both thumbs
2. deep pool	6. a sick coed	10. raise zebras
3. roommate	7. eat tomatoes	11. rob banks
4. give Valentines	8. big gamble	12. race sailboats

2. LISTEN AND PRACTICE.   Listen and repeat the phrases. Then choose four and say them out loud. Hold the last consonant of the first word until you say the next word. Do not release the last consonant strongly.

1. match' book	5. contest' prize	9. surprised' skier
2. lives' dangerously	6. aged' gracefully	10. jumped' quickly
3. change' clothes	7. fox' trails	11. laughed' crazily
4. bird' bath	8. bridge' toll	12. walked' slowly

(S) 3. LISTEN AND PRACTICE. Listen and repeat the phrases. Then choose four and say them out loud. Join final consonants to beginning vowels.

1. expert advice
2. finished early
3. complex analysis
4. turned away

5. correct answer
6. laughed aloud
7. months ago
8. piles of paper

9. picked it up
10. large apples
11. helped a student
12. a month earlier

4. APPLYING THE RULE. The bold-faced letters represent final clusters that have two or more consonants. Decide whether and how the clusters can be simplified. Then choose a sentence and read it out loud.

1. He brea**thes** too irregularly.

   "Breathes" can be simplified to "breeze," with a long "z."

2. We all brought gi**fts** for my dad's birthday.

3. The gue**sts** arri**ved** four mo**nths** ago and they still haven't left!

4. I a**sked** my boss for a raise; he a**nswered** me with a shake of his head.

5. The responsibility re**sts** with you.

(headphones) 5. QUESTIONS AND ANSWERS. Listen and repeat the expressions below. Then choose an expression and ask a classmate to define it using a complete sentence. Ask your question with *What*. Pay attention to how the final and beginning consonants are pronounced.

1. health club
2. health nut
3. health food
4. large scale
5. large intestine

6. fast food
7. lunch break
8. post card
9. box seat
10. box office

Homework

1. Record the phrases and sentences in Practices 1, 2, 3, and 4.

2. Record definitions of the expressions in Practice 5.

Related Units ▶ 4, 17, 18 19, 23, 24, 26, 28, 29, 33

UNIT 31

VOWEL LENGTH AND REDUCTION

In English, vowels in stressed syllables are usually louder and longer than vowels in unstressed syllables. Listen to the stressed syllables in these words.

to d a y   s t u dent   w o n derful

In English, many unstressed vowels are reduced to an [ə] or [ɪ] sound. Unstressed vowels may be spelled with different letters, but they are usually pronounced the same. The reduction of unstressed vowels is very important in English pronunciation. In the words below, the unstressed vowels are spelled differently but pronounced the same (as [ə]). Listen to the unstressed vowels.

l e sson   c h i cken   n a tion   o r gan
[ə]   [ə]   [ə]   [ə]

Practice

1. LISTEN AND PRACTICE. Listen and repeat the words. Then choose two from each column and say them out loud. Hold the stressed vowels to make them long. (The line means the vowel is long and stressed; ‿ means the vowel is short and unstressed.)

1. w e dding	8. o c c u r	15. to m o rrow	22. p r e sident
2. p r o mise	9. de l a y	16. e l e c tion	23. b e a u tiful
3. t r a vel	10. a r r i ve	17. pro f e ssor	24. a ccident
4. h a ppen	11. to d a y	18. re m e m ber	25. n a tional
5. d o c tor	12. a r o und	19. de v e l op	26. d i fficult
6. b r e a k fast	13. a f r a id	20. im p o r tant	27. g o vernment
7. p r o blem	14. de c i d e	21. a n o ther	28. w o n derful

2. LISTEN AND PRACTICE. Listen and repeat the words. Then choose three from each set and say them out loud. Do not pronounce the unstressed vowels with the full vowel sound. Reduce the vowel to [ə] or [ɪ].

    1. Unstressed *to-*: **to**day, **to**morrow, **to**night, **to**gether, **to**mato
        [tə]

    2. Unstressed *i*: accident, beautiful, criminal, difficult
        [ə] or [ɪ]

    3. Unstressed *-ance, -ence*: dist**ance**, entr**ance**, sil**ence**, import**ance**
        [ənts] or [əns]

    4. Unstressed *-ace, -ice, -ise, -ous*: pal**ace**, pract**ice**, prom**ise**, jeal**ous**
        [əs] or [ɪs]

    5. Unstressed *o*: police, polite, o'clock, lesson, continue, revolution
        [ə]

3. SOUNDS AND SPELLING. Listen and repeat the words in the sets below. If the bold-faced letter is pronounced as a full vowel, write the word in Column A. If it has a reduced pronunciation, write the word in Column B. When you finish writing the words, choose two from each column and say them out loud. Make the full vowels long. Pronounce the reduced vowels with [ə] or [ɪ].

1. Letter *o*

pr**o**fit pr**o**fessional **o**ccasion **o**rgan p**o**lite p**o**etry p**o**litics p**o**llution

A FULL VOWEL	B REDUCED VOWEL
profit	

2. Letter *i*

pol**i**ce pract**i**ce def**i**ne def**i**nition d**i**scuss d**i**shes m**i**stake m**i**ster

A FULL VOWEL	B REDUCED VOWEL

3. Letter *a*

parent parade material matter potato chocolate island demand

A FULL VOWEL	B REDUCED VOWEL

4. Letter *e*

decent decide residence immense elect elbow seldom select

A FULL VOWEL	B REDUCED VOWEL

4. **WORD SETS.** Listen to the words in each set. Put a line over each stressed vowel to show that it is lengthened, and put an [ə] or [ɪ] under each unstressed vowel to show it is reduced. Choose a set and write a sentence using all the words in the set, adding words when you need to. Underline thought groups so you can read your sentence smoothly. Then read your sentence out loud.

Example: dangerous, accident, Washington
[ə][ə] [ə][ə] [ɪ] [ə]
There was a dangerous accident in Washington.

1. o'clock, tomorrow, practice, guitar

2. beautiful, entrance, office

(continued on next page)

3. today, lesson, difficult

_____

4. police, weapon, dangerous, criminal

_____

Homework

1. Record the words in Practices 1 and 2. Lengthen stressed vowels and reduce unstressed vowels.

2. Write sentences for all of the word sets in Practice 4 and record them. Speak slowly. Lengthen stressed vowels and reduce unstressed vowels.

Related Units ▶ 3, 5, 6, 10, 18, 24, 32, 33, 35, 36, 37, 38

UNIT 32

STRESS RULES FOR SUFFIXES

When most prefixes and suffixes are added to form new words, the stressed syllable in the new word is the same as the stressed syllable in the base word.

estáblish	estáblishment
cléver	cléverness
ángry	ángrily
áble	unáble
desígn	desígner

However, when some suffixes are added, the stress shifts to a different syllable. Study these rules.

■ When *-tion, -sion, -ic, -ical, -ically, -ity, -ian, -ial, -ialize, -ious, -graphy,* and *-logy* are added to words, stress usually falls on the syllable just before the suffix. (Secondary stress, written `, is described below.)

defíne	dèfinítion	psychólogy	psychológical
fántasy	fàntástic	télegràph	telégraphy

■ When *-ese, -eer/-ier,* and sometimes *-ee* are added to a word, stress usually shifts to the suffix.

Chína Chìnése	Japán Jàpanése

■ The verbs endings *-ate* and *-ize* have secondary stress. Primary stress usually falls two syllables to the left of the *-ate* or *-ize* ending.

óperàte	réalìze

■ When a word ending in *-ate* is used as a noun or adjective, *-ate* does not usually have secondary stress and its pronunciation is reduced to [ət].

VERB: [eyt]	NOUN/ADJECTIVE: [ət]
to dúplicàte	a dúplicate copy
to gráduàte	gráduate school
to éstimàte	an éstimate

■ When primary stress falls on or after the third syllable, there is often a secondary stress two syllables to the left. Syllables with secondary stress have full vowels and are long. They do not, however, have high pitch like primary stressed syllables.

còntribútion   Jàpanése   rèalístic

Practice

1. APPLYING THE RULE. Listen and repeat the first word. Mark the vowel with primary stress. Then mark primary and secondary stress on the other words in the set. Choose a set and say all the words out loud.

1. compéte   còmpetítion, compétitive
2. edit   editor, editorial, editorialize
3. commerce   commercial, commercialization, commercially
4. public   publicity, publicize
5. photograph   photography, photographic, photographer
6. profit   profiteer, profitable, profitability
7. mountain   mountainous, mountaineer
8. objective   objectify, objectivity
9. minor   minority
10. person   personify, personification
11. circulate   circulatory, circulation
12. finance   financial, financier

2. DIALOGUES. Work in pairs to complete the dialogues. Use the appropriate form of the word in parentheses to respond to all of the questions in a set. Mark stress on that word. Practice reading the dialogues with your partner.

1. (circulate)

    a. A: If your fingers and feet are always cold, you probably have poor . . . what's it called?

        B: _____ Cìrculátion _____.

    b. A: What does blood do as it travels through the blood vessels?

        B: _____ .

    c. A: What adjective describes the body's system of blood vessels and blood?

        B: The _____ system.

2. (mountain)

    a. A: How would you describe the state of Alaska?

        B: _____ .

    b. A: What's a term for a person who lives and works in the mountains?

        B: A _____ .

3. (edit)

    a. A: What should you do before turning in a piece of written work?

        B: _____ it.

    b. A: What do you call newspaper articles that are intended to express the writer's opinion?

        B: _____ .

    c. A: On a newspaper, who makes the decision to print a particular story or not?

        B: The _____ .

4. (compete)

    a. A: When runners race against each other, what are they doing?

        B: They're _____ .

    b. A: In a pure capitalist system, what must be present?

        B: Free _____ among businesses.

    c. A: Why do brothers and sisters sometimes feel jealous of each other?

        B: They're _____ .

🎧 **3. APPLYING THE RULE.** Listen and repeat the pairs of words with *-ate*. Then fill in the blanks with the word in parentheses and its pronunciation, [eyt] or [ət]. Choose two sentences and read them out loud. Be sure to pronounce the *-ate* ending correctly.

1. to duplicate   a duplicate   4. to estimate   an estimate
2. to associate   an associate   5. to separate   a separate room
3. to graduate   a graduate   6. to alternate   an alternate

1. (duplicate)

    a. I don't know whether he wants the original or a _____*duplicate* [ət]_____ .

    b. If he wants a _____ , I'll have to _____ the original.

2. (associate) After discussing the case with my _____ , I have decided

    not to _____ with the man.

3. (graduate) When you _____ from college, do you want to go to

    _____ school?

4. (estimate) I asked the mechanic to _____ the cost of fixing the car,

    but his _____ was much too high.

5. Make your own sentences for *separate* and *alternate*.

    _____ .

    _____ .

Homework

1. Record the words in Practices 1 and 3.

2. Make one or two sentences for each of these word sets.

    a. photograph, photography, photographer

    b. electric, electricity, electrification

    c. separate (verb), separate (noun/adjective)

    d. public, publicity, publicize

Related Units ▶ 5, 6, 31, 33

UNIT 33

STRESS PATTERNS

■ Compound nouns are two nouns used together as one noun, such as *railroad.* Compounds have a special stress-pitch pattern. Primary stress and high pitch fall on the first noun; secondary stress and low pitch fall on the second noun. Listen to the compounds.

post office   railroad   school bus

■ Some other two-word sequences can also have the stress-pitch pattern of noun compounds. When separable two-word verbs like *take off* or *make up* are used as nouns, they have the same stress-pitch pattern as noun compounds. Listen to the phrases.

The takeoff has been delayed an hour.   I bought some new makeup.

■ Some words change their grammatical category when the stress pattern is changed. For example, a word like *récord,* stressed on the first syllable, is a noun. If stress shifts to the second syllable, *recórd,* the word becomes a verb. Listen to the pairs. The vowel without primary stress may either be reduced (to [ə]) or pronounced with secondary stress.

NOUN	VERB
record	record
convict	convict
present	present

Spelling and other details

▶ Some noun compounds are written as one word, without a space between the two nouns: *railroad, bedroom, roommate, bookstore.*

▶ Other noun compounds are written as separate words: *library book, hair stylist, bus route.*

(S)

1. APPLYING THE RULE. Listen and repeat the compound words. Review the rules for final consonants below and decide how the consonants at the end of the words are pronounced.

- If the final consonant of the first word and the beginning consonant of the second word are the same, put a line above the two consonants to show one long consonant: roo͞omate.

- If a vowel begins the next word, underline the joining: car‿engine.

- If a different consonant begins the next word, mark the final consonant with ' to show it is unreleased: chalk' board.

1. post‿office
2. graduate school
3. White House
4. age limit
5. travel agent
6. popcorn
7. rocket ship
8. greenhouse
9. footbridge
10. orange juice
11. driver's license
12. darkroom
13. report card
14. shopping mall

Now choose three and say them out loud. Pronounce the stress-pitch pattern correctly.

2. QUESTIONS AND ANSWERS. Choose a compound from Practice 1 and ask a classmate to define it using a complete sentence. Ask your question with *What*. Pay attention to final consonants and pronounce the stress-pitch pattern correctly.

3. LISTEN AND PRACTICE. Listen and repeat the word pairs. Mark primary stress, secondary stress, and reduced vowels. Then choose three pairs and say them out loud.

NOUN	VERB
1. a. a cónvèrt	b. to convért
	[ə]
2. a. a record	b. to record
3. a. a rebel	b. to rebel
4. a. a suspect	b. to suspect
5. a. a convict	b. to convict

6. a. your conduct		b. to conduct
7. a. a present		b. to present
8. a. the object		b. to object
9. a. a contract		b. to contract
10. a. a protest		b. to protest

4. HEARING DIFFERENCES. Listen and repeat the words. Circle the stress pattern.

1. convict	noun	verb
2. object	noun	verb
3. conduct	noun	verb
4. present	noun	verb
5. contract	noun	verb
6. rebel	noun	verb
7. record	noun	verb

Homework

1. Record the words in Practices 1 and 3.

2. A new town is going to be built. You are one of the town planners, and you are in charge of planning five buildings or services. You can choose from the list below or think of your own. Describe the five buildings or services you are in charge of: what they will look like, who will use them, and so on. Use compound intonation when appropriate (all of the phrases below are compounds).

post office	drugstore	supermarket	office building
parking lot	skating rink	sport stadium	swimming pool
police station	medical clinic	schoolhouse	lending library
department store	courthouse	fish market	movie theater

Related Units ▶ 5, 6, 17, 30, 31, 32

UNIT 34

RHYTHM, THOUGHT GROUPS, AND IMPORTANT WORDS

🎧 Rhythm

Rhythm is the alternation of strong (stressed) and weak (unstressed) syllables. Correct rhythm will make your speech smoother and easier to understand. Listen to Robert the Robot say the same greeting two ways: *I'm Robert the Robot, at your service. I'll talk to you whenever you're lonely.* Describe the difference between the two. Which robot would you rather have in your home?

🎧 Thought Groups

Dividing sentences into thought groups helps the listener organize the meaning of the sentence. Thought groups also help the speaker by breaking long stretches of speech into shorter ones.

Certain rhythm patterns are common to particular types of phrases. The phrases are often thought groups themselves. The rhythm pattern of prepositional phrases, for example, is a weak beat (the preposition) followed by a strong beat (the noun). Verbs followed by object pronouns are an example of a strong beat (the verb) followed by a weak beat (the pronoun). Listen to the rhythm of these phrases.

Wĕak Stróng:	ăt tén	ĭn Júne	tŏ scʹhool
Stróng Wĕak:	brʹing ĭt	tʹake thĕm	cʹall hĕr

Listen to the thought groups in this sentence.

The taxi driver brought us to the airport at ten o'clock in the morning.

∩ Important Words

In most sentences, one word is more important than the others. The context of
the sentence determines which word (sometimes words) is most important,
and speakers usually highlight the word by pronouncing it on a high pitch.
Listen to the pitch of the bold-faced words in these sentences.

We **have** to move this weekend. There's no other **time** to do it.

Practice

1. HEARING RHYTHM.   Listen and repeat the dialogue. Mark weak or unstressed
syllables (with ˘) and strong or stressed syllables (with ´). Underline thought groups and
circle the most important word(s). Then practice reading the dialogue with a partner.
What do you notice about the rhythm patterns of the four different lines?

> Customer: I'm (ready) to order.
>
> Waiter: The chicken is yummy.
>
> Customer: I think I'll have waffles.
>
> Waiter: The waffles are awful!

2. THE RHYTHM GAME.   Work as a class. Take turns making sentences that begin
with the letters of the alphabet. Every sentence should end with a word that has the same
rhythm pattern as *apple.* Use dictionaries if necessary. Then do a class reading of the
alphabet sentences. Use high pitch on the last word.

> *Example:*   *A is for apple.*
>
> *B is for* _____ baby _____ .

3. DIALOGUES.   Listen and repeat the first three lines of the dialogues below. Circle
the most important word in each line. Then, with a partner, complete the last line of each
dialogue choosing a word or words with the same stress pattern as the preceding lines.
Practice reading the dialogues with your partner.

1. A: What's the matter?
   B: There's no water.
   A: Call the plumber.
   B: What's his _____ ?

2. A: I need your help to fix the car.
   B: I'll come tonight at ten o'clock.
   A: You said before you'd come at nine.
   B: I'm busy then. I'll come _____ .

4. QUESTIONS AND ANSWERS.   Write an answer to each question, using a complete sentence. Circle the most important word (the word that expresses the new information). Then ask a question and choose a classmate to answer it. Use high pitch on the most important word.

> *Example: What's the tallest mountain in the world?*
> <u>Mount Everest is the tallest mountain in the world.</u>

1. What's the largest country in the world (largest in area)?

   _____

2. What's the largest state in the United States?

   _____

3. What's the longest river in the world?

   _____

4. What's the largest mammal in the world?

   _____

5. What's the largest land mammal in the world?

   _____

6. What's the most populous state in the United States?

   _____

7. What's the longest river in the United States?

   _____

8. What's the largest country in South America (largest in area)?

   _____

9. What's the most populous country in the world?

   _____

10. What's the tallest mountain in the United States?

   _____

Homework

1. Record the dialogue in Practice 1.

2. Write a sentence for every letter of the alphabet, using Practice 2 as a model. Make sure each sentence ends with the same rhythm pattern. Record the sentences, using high pitch on the last word.

Related Units ▶ 5, 6, 31, 32, 33, 35, 36, 37, 38

UNIT 35

COMMON REDUCED WORDS

Some words are reduced in normal speaking.

- **And.** In normal speaking, the word *and* is unstressed and pronounced [ən], without final [d]. It sounds like the ending of *given* and is joined to the preceding word. (Sometimes it is written *'n'* to show its reduced pronunciation.)

  strong_and weak   tall_and short   paper_and pencil

- **Or.** In normal speaking, the word *or* is unstressed and pronounced [ər], like the *-er* ending of *bigger*. *Or* is joined to the preceding word.

  right_or wrong   big_or small   rain_or snow

- **Can/Can't.** When the word *can* occurs inside a sentence, it is unstressed and pronounced [kn], like the ending of *chicken*. If you stress *can* or use the full vowel [æ], your listener may think you have said *can't*.

  Cho_can cook chicken.   Max_can play the piano.
      [kn]   [kn]

  Use the stressed full vowel when you say *can't* and when you use *can* in a short answer.

  I cán't do this homework.   We cán't go.   Yes, I cán.
  [kænt]   [kænt]   [kæn]

Practice

1. LISTEN AND PRACTICE.   Listen and repeat the words and phrases with *and*. Then choose three sets and say them out loud. The single word and the underlined noun + *and* have the same pronunciation.

1. redden   red and white   4. fallen   fall and get up

2. deaden   dead and buried   5. given   give and take

3. often*   off and on   6. eaten   eat and drink

* The *t* in *often* is silent: *offen.*

(S) 2. LISTEN AND PRACTICE. Listen and repeat the words and phrases with *or*. Then choose three sets and say them out loud. The single word and the underlined noun + *or* have the same pronunciation.

1. blacker   black or white
2. happier   happy or sad
3. runner   run or walk
4. worker   work or play
5. buyer   buy or sell
6. cleaner   clean or dirty

(S) 3. LISTEN AND PRACTICE. Listen and repeat the words and sentences with *can*. Then choose three sets and say them out loud. The single word and the underlined subject + *can* have the same pronunciation.

1. weaken   We can go.
2. awaken   A way can be found.
3. bacon   Mr. Bay can come.
4. beacon   Bea can speak French.

4. HEARING DIFFERENCES. Listen to the phrases and fill in the blanks with *and* or *or*.

1. red _____ white
2. red _____ black
3. come _____ go
4. lunch _____ dinner
5. mother _____ father
6. land _____ sea

5. HEARING DIFFERENCES. Listen to the sentences and fill in the blanks with *can* or *can't*.

1. She _____ swim.
2. Juan _____ drive.
3. Don't call me if you _____ come.
4. Don't call me if you _____ come.
5. I _____ go this weekend.
6. I _____ bring it to you later.

6. MEANING DIFFERENCES. Work in pairs. Pronounce *can* or *can't* correctly, so your partner knows how to respond. Look at the two examples.

Example: Alice: *Bob, I wanted to tell you that I* __can__ *come to your party this*
[kn]
Saturday.

Bob: *Oh, I'm so glad!*

OR

Alice: *Bob, I wanted to tell you that I* __can't__ *come to your party this*
[kænt]
Saturday.

Bob: *Oh, I'm so disappointed!*

1. come to your party this Saturday
2. give you a ride home tonight
3. fix your TV this weekend
4. teach you how to swim this summer
5. lend you the money you need
6. teach you the tango tomorrow
7. repay the money I borrowed from you
8. go to the beach with you this afternoon

7. INTERVIEWS.

Interview a classmate to find out his or her skills. Ask questions with *can*. Some abilities are listed below, but you can add to them. Report your information to the class using *can* or *can't*.

Sports and Physical Activities: swim from Florida to Cuba, swim partway from

Florida to Cuba, play _____ , scuba dive, dance, sky dive

Skills: type, change a tire, fix a lamp, turn on a lamp, drive, fly an airplane, cook

_____ food

Languages: speak _____ , write _____

Homework

1. Record the words, phrases, and sentences in Practices 1, 2, and 3.

2. Record four sentences, each of which describes two skills you have. Use *can* and *and* in your sentences, with the reduced pronunciation of these words.

Example: ___I can play tennis and volleyball.___
[kn]   [ən]

Then record four sentences, each of which describes two skills you do not have. Use *can't* and *or* in your sentences, with the reduced pronunciation of *or*.

Example: ___I can't speak Russian or German.___
[ər]

Related Units ▶ 5, 6, 10, 31, 32, 33, 34, 36, 37, 38

UNIT 36

CONTRACTIONS

Use contractions when you speak. Your English will sound more natural and "friendly."

■ Contractions with *am, is, are.*

> **I'm** a student.
> **She's** an artist.
> **John's** an engineer.
> **You're** late.
> **They're** here.

- When *are* occurs after a noun (not the pronouns *you, we, they*), it is pronounced like an *-er* ending to that word.

> You and **Max're** from Boston. (say "maxer")
>
> **Ships're** large boats. (say "shipser")

- When *is* is contracted with a noun ending in [s, z, ʃ, ʒ, tʃ, dʒ], it is pronounced like the plural ending.

> The **rose's** red. (say "roses")
>
> The **church's** beautiful. (say "churches")

■ Contractions with *had, would.*

- Do not release the contracted [d] when the next word begins with a consonant.

> **I'd**⁾ better go.
>
> **He'd**⁾ like a hamburger.
>
> **They'd**⁾ rather drive.

- When *had* and *would* are contracted after words ending in [d, t], they are pronounced as an [əd] ending (like the past tense ending of verbs ending in [t, d]). (*Had* and *would* are usually written in full form in these cases.)

> **Dad'd** like chicken. (say "dádded")

■ Contractions with *will*.

> **I'll** be at home.   **You'll** like the movie.
> **She'll** call tonight.   **They'll** be late.

- When *will* is contracted after full nouns (not pronouns), it loses [w] and is pronounced as a final syllable [əl] with the preceding word.

> The **bank'll** be closed tomorrow. (say "bánkul")

■ Contractions with *not*.

- Do not release the [t] of *n't* when the next word begins with a consonant.

> That **isn't⁾** right.   I **wouldn't⁾** do that if I were you.
>
> They **aren't⁾** pleased.   They **weren't⁾** clean.
>
> She **won't⁾** go.   It **doesn't⁾** matter.

■ Do not contract *am, is, are, had, will,* and *would* when these words end a sentence or a clause. When *am, is, are, had, will,* and *would* end a sentence or clause, they are stressed.

> Yes, I am. (~~Yes, I'm.~~)   I will if you will. (~~I'll if you'll.~~)
>
> Yes, he is. (~~Yes, he's.~~)   Would you like a ride? Yes, I would. (~~Yes, I'd.~~)

Practice

1. LISTEN AND PRACTICE.   Listen and repeat the sentences. Then choose three and say them out loud.

1. I'm Íma.
2. You're Yúri.
3. They're thére.
4. He's Éaz.
5. We're weírd.
6. It's ítsy.

2. QUESTIONS AND ANSWERS. Listen and repeat the questions in Column A. Use rising intonation on the tag question (*isn't it?*). Listen and repeat the answers in Column B. Match the questions in Column A with the answers in Column B. Then ask a question from Column A and choose a classmate to answer it.

A	B
1. Disney World's in Miami, isn't it?	a. No, it isn't. It's in Philadelphia.
2. The Statue of Liberty's in Washington, D.C., isn't it?	b. No, it isn't. It's in Orlando.
	c. No, it isn't. It's in Seattle.
3. Fisherman's Wharf's in Los Angeles, isn't it?	d. No, it isn't. It's in San Antonio.
	e. No, it isn't. It's in Cambridge.
4. The Liberty Bell's in Chicago, isn't it?	f. No, it isn't. It's in New Orleans.
5. Harvard's in Boston, isn't it?	g. No, it isn't. It's in Washington, D.C.
6. The Latin Quarter's in Seattle, isn't it?	h. No, it isn't. It's in Chicago.
7. The Sears Tower's in New York, isn't it?	i. No, it isn't. It's in San Francisco.
	j. No, it isn't. It's in New York.
8. The Pentagon's in Baltimore, isn't it?	
9. The Space Needle's in Phoenix, isn't it?	
10. The Alamo's in Houston, isn't it?	

3. QUESTIONS AND ANSWERS. Listen and repeat the questions. Write a two-sentence answer for each question. The first sentence will be a short *yes-no* answer. The sentences should include contractions when possible. Then ask a question and choose a classmate to answer it.

Examples: *Are you tired?* __Yes, I ám. I'm álways tired.__

Will you open the window? __No, I wón't. It's cóld.__

1. Is dinner ready?

_____

2. Are you cold?

_____

3. Will you be home tonight?

_____

4. Did you buy the book I wanted?

_____

5. Have you seen _____"The Godfather"_____ ?

6. Are they coming?

_____

4. DIALOGUES.   Listen to the example. Then work in pairs to complete the dialogues. Practice reading the dialogues out loud, using intonation to show strong feeling.

Example: A: *Would you like some snails?*

             B: *No, I wouldn't! I'd rather eat* _____ *worms* _____ !

1. A: Would you like some frogs' legs?

   B: No, I wouldn't! I'd rather eat _____ !

2. A: Would you like some brains?

   B: No, I wouldn't! I'd rather eat _____ !

5. INTERVIEWS.   Interview a classmate. Find out at least four pieces of information about your classmate. Take notes. Report the information to the class, using contractions when possible. Speak as smoothly and clearly as you can.

Example: ___Maria's from Ecuador. She's been here for six___

               ___months. She's studying English and ballet. She'd___

               ___like to be a dancer. She'll apply for jobs next year.___

Notes: from Ecuador   studying English and ballet
             6 months   dancer
                              apply for jobs next year

Homework

1. Record the sentences in Practice 1.

2. Record some information about one of your classmates, using contractions when you can. (You can use your notes from Practice 5.)

Related Units ▶ 4, 5, 6, 10, 17, 30, 31, 32, 34, 35, 39, 40

UNIT 37

PREPOSITIONS

🎧 ■ In prepositional phrases, most short prepositions are not stressed. The vowel may be reduced, while the vowel in the following noun is stressed and long. Listen to the rhythm pattern of these phrases.

in a minute   to school   at night

on time   for a year   with a friend

■ Some short prepositions are pronounced with a reduced vowel. Listen to the full vowel of the preposition in its word-list pronunciation and the reduced vowel in normal speaking.

FULL VOWEL (WORD LIST)		REDUCED VOWEL (NORMAL SPEAKING)	
át	[æt]	at hóme	[ət]
tó	[tuw]	to the móvies	[tə]
fór	[for]	for a whíle	[fər]

■ When words such as *to, on,* or *in* end a sentence, they are not reduced and have a longer vowel. Listen.

I want tó.   Come ón.   Go ín.

■ Short words that are part of separable two-word verbs are usually stressed. Listen.

pick it úp   try it ón   throw it óut

■ There are some special rules for *to. To* is often pronounced with the full vowel [uw] when the next word begins with a vowel, especially when that vowel is not stressed. Listen to these phrases.

FULL VOWEL: [uw]	REDUCED VOWEL: [ə]
to_a friend	to the friend
to_another	to the other
to_enjoy	to go
to_agree	to do

Practice

1. LISTEN AND PRACTICE. Listen and repeat the prepositional phrases. Then choose five and say them out loud. Don't stress the preposition. Make the vowel of the noun long.

1. at home
2. at ten
3. at the gym
4. on the weekend
5. on time
6. on Monday
7. for class
8. for students
9. for_a year
10. for dinner
11. to the park
12. to_a bank
13. to school
14. in Texas
15. in_a minute
16. in_a hurry

2. IDIOMS AND EXPRESSIONS. Listen and repeat the prepositional phrases in Column B. Pronounce the joinings and don't release consonants followed by the unreleased symbol ʾ. Then match the questions in Column A with the phrases in Column B. Read a question and ask a classmate to answer it.

A	B
1. What's an idiom that means "immediately"?	a. for the time being
2. When is the sun directly overhead?	b. in_a nutshell
3. What's an idiom that means "always active"?	c. atʾ once
4. What's an idiom that means "permanently"?	d. in_a minute
5. What's an idiom that means "free after an escape"?	e. atʾ large
6. What's an idiom that means "for now"?	f. in_a jam
7. Where's Phoenix?	g. on the go
8. What's an idiom that means "in trouble"?	h. atʾ noon
9. What's an idiom that means "in summary" or "in a few words?"	i. for good
	j. in_Arizona
10. It's 3:00 now. When will it be 3:01*?	

* Read "three-oh-one."

3. LISTEN AND PRACTICE.   Listen and repeat these phrases where the short word is stressed. Then choose three and say them out loud.

1. finish up
2. come on
3. climbed up
4. hand it in

5. clean it up
6. turned it on
7. throw it out
8. go in

9. look out
10. go on
11. try it on
12. picked it up

4. SPEAKING.   First listen and repeat the phrases below. Then work in pairs. Student A describes a picture while Student B draws it (don't show your partner the picture). Use prepositional phrases in your description, and make it as complete as possible. Then switch roles. (Student A's picture is on page 151; Student B's picture is on page 154.)

1. on the right side
2. in the middle
3. in the upper left corner

4. in the lower right corner
5. at the top
6. at the bottom

Homework

1. Record the phrases in Practices 1 and 3.

2. Make a one-minute recording of a frightening experience you've had. Use prepositional phrases to describe where and when it happened.

Related Units ▶ 5, 6, 10, 17, 31, 32, 34, 35, 38

UNIT 38

PRONOUNS

Personal pronouns (*I, me, you, he, him, she, her, it, we, us, they, them*) are normally unstressed in English. Listen.

> I'm cóld. Can you clóse the wíndow?
>
> When they fínish the létter, téll them to sénd it expréss.

■ Pronouns starting with *h*.

When the pronouns *he, him,* and *her* occur inside a phrase, the *h* is often dropped and the rest of the pronoun joins to the preceding word. Listen.

> What did h̸e do? ("Did h̸e" is pronounced like "diddy.")
>
> After you cáll h̸im, téll h̸er what h̸e sáid.
>
>> ("Call h̸im" is pronounced like "callim"; "tell h̸er" is pronounced like "teller"; "what h̸e" is pronounced like "whatty.")

■ Personal pronoun *it*.

When *it* is the object of a verb, it is usually joined to the preceding word. Listen.

> Thrów it.   Cátch it.   Dó it.

■ Pronoun reductions in fast speech.

In fast speech, many English-speakers make pronoun reductions, which you should be aware of. If you are not a fluent speaker of English, you should not try to make these reductions yourself.

- When *you* is preceded by a word ending in *d*, it often joins with the end of the word to make a [dʒ] sound. Listen.

> Did you go? ("Did you" is pronounced like "didja.")

- When *you* is preceded by a word ending in *t*, it often joins with the end of the word to make a [tʃ] sound. Listen.

    They won't let you do it. ("Let you" is pronounced like "letcha.")

- When *you* is preceded by a word ending in a vowel, it is often pronounced as [yə]. Listen.

    See you tomorrow. ("See you" is pronounced like "seeya.")

- When *them* is the object of a verb, it is often pronounced as an ending to the verb without the beginning "th" sound. Listen.

    You'll find them in the closet. ("Find them" is pronounced like "findum.")

Practice

1. LISTEN AND PRACTICE.   Listen and repeat the sentences. Use high pitch and strong stress on the bold-faced words. Underline thought groups. Then choose four lines and read them with a partner. What do you think A has lost?

1. A: I'm **sure** I had it this **morning**.

2. B: I **can't** believe it! This is the **second** time this week!

3. A: No, no, it's **not**. It happened **last** week, **too**.

4. B: Well, it's **got** to be here **somewhere**. Did you check your pockets?

5. A: Well, of **course**! That's the **first** place I looked.

6. B: The **only** solution is for you to **put** it on a string and **wear** it around your **neck**!

7. A: I **can't** do that until I **find** it!

8. B: Look in **here**, Josh. We've got a **real problem**.

9. A: **Oh no**! I've locked them **inside**!

10. B: **Now** what are we going to do?

2. QUESTIONS AND ANSWERS.   Read the questions and write answers using an *h* pronoun. If the pronoun occurs after a word, draw a line though the *h* and an underline to join it to the preceding word. Then ask a question and choose a classmate to answer it.

Example: *How do you feel about the president of the United States?*

I like ̸him. I think ̸he's doing a good job.

1. According to the official record, what did Lee Harvey Oswald do to John F. Kennedy?

   _____

2. The mall security guard discovered the little boy who had been separated from his mother and who was crying. How did the guard help the little boy?

   _____

3. The woman went to the hospital emergency room complaining of severe stomach pain. What did the doctors do for the woman?

   _____

4. You are in a strange city and you're trying to find your hotel. You see a friendly looking policeman on the corner. What do you do?

   _____

5. Your mother's birthday is next week, but you can't be there. What should you do?

   _____

6. John forgot his anniversary and his wife is very upset. He wants to set things right between them. What should he do?

   _____

3. THE PRONOUN GAME.   Think of a thing that can be used. Write down several verbs that describe how it is used. Give your classmates clues to help them guess the name of the thing. Use pronouns when you give clues.

   Example: I'm thinking of something that's oval shaped. You

   can eat it. If you drop it, it'll break. What is it?

4. SPEAKING.   Work in pairs. You and your partner have been invited to go before the Complaint Board and air your complaints about each other. Choose a pair from the list below and decide what you don't like about each other. You will make your complaint to the Complaint Board and not directly to your partner. Use pronouns and start your complaint this way: "I want to make a complaint about my _____ . I don't like it when he/she . . . ."

> Example: Husband: *I want to make a complaint about* <u>my wife</u> *. I don't like it*
>
> *when she* <u>pretends she doesn't hear me</u> *.*
>
> Wife: *I want to make a complaint about* <u>my husband</u> *. I don't*
>
> *like it when he* <u>talks so much</u> *.*

1. a husband and wife
2. a teacher and student
3. a boss and employee
4. a parent and child

5. two roommates
6. two classmates
7. a boyfriend and girlfriend
8. two best friends

Homework

1. Record the dialogue in Practice 1.

2. Make a one-minute recording about a time when you lost something. Use pronouns when you can.

Related Units ▶ 5, 6, 10, 27, 31, 32, 35, 36

UNIT 39

EXPANDING VOICE RANGE

Intonation is the melody or song of speech. Intonation can tell your listener if you are happy or sad, bored or interested, certain or uncertain. It is very important to use the full range of your voice when you speak. If you speak with a "flat" intonation, your listener may think you are bored and uninterested or even unfriendly.

Practice

1. LISTEN AND PRACTICE. Listen to the dialogue below. Then circle the words that describe how A feels about B. In what situation might this dialogue take place? What might A say next?

A: What are you doing here?

B: I'm waiting for a bus.

A: The bus doesn't stop here.

B: No?

A's feelings toward B: friendly   surprised   suspicious   unfriendly

Now listen to the dialogue again. Circle the words that describe how A feels about B. In what situation might *this* dialogue take place? What might A say next?

A: What are you doing here?

B: I'm waiting for a bus.

A: The bus doesn't stop here.

B: No?

A's feelings toward B: friendly   surprised   suspicious   unfriendly

Work with a partner. Decide how A and B feel about each other. Then practice the dialogue using intonation to show that feeling.

🎧 **2. DIALOGUES.** In the dialogues below, A is offering to do something for B. B's intonation shows that B believes A's offer is impossible. Listen to the example. Practice the dialogues with a partner, using the same intonation patterns. Then write your own dialogue and practice it with a partner.

> *Example:* A: *Would you like a ride?*
>
> B: *You don't have a car.*

1. A: Would you like to go to a steak house for dinner?

   B: You don't eat meat.

2. A: Can I help you with your calculus homework?

   B: You've never taken calculus.

3. A: Shall we go to a baseball game?

   B: You don't like sports.

4. A: _____?

   B: _____.

🔊 **3. EXPANDING VOICE RANGE.** Listen to the example. Work in pairs to complete the dialogues. Use the word(s) in parentheses to respond to all of the questions in a set. Use strong intonation to show strong feelings. Practice the dialogues with your partner.

> *Example:* *(milk)*
>
> a. A: *Milk is the most unhealthy food in the world.*
>
> B: _____Milk_____ *!!!???*
>
> b. A: *What important food product comes from cows?*
>
> B: _____Milk_____ .
>
> c. A: *I'm thinking of something people drink. What is it?*
>
> B: _____Milk_____ ?

1. (English)

   a. A: What language do most people in England speak?

   B: _____ .

b. A: In the year 2050, what will the dominant language of the United States be?

B: _____?

c. A: Half the people in Brazil are native speakers of English.

B: _____!!!???

2. (on the table)

a. A: I put the sofa on the table.

B: _____!!!???

b. A: Where did I leave my keys?

B: I don't know. _____?

c. A: Where do you want me to put your books?

B: There. _____.

Homework

1. Record the dialogues in Practice 3.

2. Write short responses to the situations below and record your responses. Use intonation to show your reaction.

   Example: *Your best friend comes to you, looking very upset. He/she tells you that his/her car has just been stolen. How do you respond?*

   Oh no! Are you sure?? What happened?!

   a. You have a headache and you're very tired. You have just arrived at home and all you can think of is sleep. Your roommate suddenly bursts into your room and says that you must get up now and do the dishes. How do you respond?

   _____

   _____

   b. Your parents call to tell you they have just won the lottery and they are millionaires! How do you respond?

   _____

   _____

Related Units ▶ 6, 9, 14, 16, 19, 21, 26, 29, 32, 40

UNIT 40

RISING AND FALLING INTONATION

Falling Intonation

Strong expectations or certainty are often shown by using a falling pitch.
Listen.

Look at that smile! You got the promotion, didn't you?   (I'm sure you did.)

- The falling intonation on the tag question (*didn't you?*) shows that the speaker expects the answer to be, "Yes, I did."

- When sentences are statements of fact or show what the speaker believes, they also end with falling intonation. Listen.

He lives on Fourth Street.

Rising Intonation

Uncertainty, or lack of expectation, is shown by using rising intonation. Listen.

I haven't heard from you in months. Everything's fine, isn't it?

- The rising intonation on the tag question (*isn't it?*) shows that the speaker is uncertain about the answer.

- *Yes-no* questions also typically end with rising intonation.

Do you have to work this weekend?   Are you hungry?

░░░░░░░░░░░░░░░Practice░░░░░░░░░░░░░░░

1. HEARING INTONATION. Listen and repeat the dialogue. Draw the intonation on the tag questions.

A: You're not going to marry that horrible man, are you?

B: I told you to stay out of my life, didn't I?

A: I've always supported your decisions before, haven't I?

B: You're in love with him yourself, aren't you?

A: Your parents don't know about him, do they?

B: You won't tell them, will you?

A: You're afraid they won't like him, aren't you?

B: I don't know what to do. Do you?

2. USING INTONATION. Imagine that last year was the coldest winter on record in Maine. Look at the sentences and decide whether they describe the Maine winter, the Florida winter, or both. Write "In Maine" or "In Florida" in the blank at the front of the sentence. At the end of the sentence, write a tag question. Decide whether the tag question should be read with a rising or falling intonation and draw it in. Then choose a sentence and read it out loud.

Example: _____In Maine_____ *, the ski resorts did well,* ___didn't they___ *?*

1. _____ , there were over 30 major snowstorms, _____ ?

2. _____ , it snowed three times, _____ ?

3. _____ , kids missed a lot of school because of the snow,

    _____ ?

4. _____ , heating bills were high this winter, _____ ?

5. _____ , Disney World remained open, _____ ?

6. _____ , a lot of people had colds or got the flu, _____ ?

7. _____ , storms canceled a lot of events, _____ ?

8. _____ , tourists hoping to escape the cold were disappointed,

    _____ ?

3. INTERVIEWS. With a partner, conduct job interviews using the Help Wanted ads and resumes below. Student A is the interviewer: Read the resume and think of questions you want to ask the applicant. Student B is the applicant: Read the Help Wanted ad and think of questions you want to ask about the job. Use appropriate intonation. Then switch roles, using the ad and resume on p. 141.

Example: Interviewer: *You have computer experience, don't you?*

Have you ever repaired mainframes?

Applicant: *I know you're looking for a repair person.*

Would I be able to learn any computer programming?

HELP WANTED

Computer repair person in growing company. Flexible hours and good pay. Some experience required but company offers on-the-job training. Good medical benefits.

RESUME

Michael Park
612 Westbrook Road
New Paltz, New York 12404
(914) 324-9877

Work Experience

1995-1996	ABC Computer Services, computer repair (part-time)
1994-1995	Joe's Diner, waiter

Education

1995-1996	State University of New York, New Paltz
1991-1995	Rondout Central Valley High School

Hobbies

Basketball, chess, hiking, playing the drums

HELP WANTED

Full-time summer job working in summer science program for junior high school girls. Job requirements include assisting classroom teachers and serving as a dormitory counselor for junior high school students. Some college required.

RESUME

Sandy Kim
819 Eastlake Drive
Seattle, Washington 98109
(206) 501-8810

Work Experience

1993-1996   Barton's Bookstore, salesperson (part-time)

Education

1994-1996   University of Washington, Seattle
1990-1994   Eisenhower High School

Hobbies
Reading, swimming

Homework

1. Record the dialogue in Practice 1.

2. Look in the Help Wanted section of a newspaper. Find a job you would be interested in. Describe what you know about the job, using falling intonation. Use rising intonation with *yes-no* questions to ask for information about the job that the ad does not tell you.

Related Units ▶ 6, 9, 14, 16, 19, 21, 26, 29, 32, 39

APPENDIX | ANSWERS AND LISTENING TEXTS

UNIT 1

Practice 1   2. show; 3. jazz; 4. weather, whether; 5. right, write; 6. book; 7. tooth; 8. singing

Practice 2   2. [θ]; 3. [z]; 4. [r]; 5. [tʃ]; 6. [f]; 7. [t]; 8. [pt]

UNIT 2

Practice 2   1. I see you.   2. Why are you sad?   3. Are you okay?   4. for you

UNIT 5

Practice 1   2. búsiness _2_ ; 3. ínterest _2_ ; 4. áspirin _2_ ; 5. fávorite _2_ ; 6. ópera _2_ ; 7. végetables _3_ ; 8. ínterested _3_ ; 9. dífferent _2_ ; 10. évening _2_ ; 11. áverage _2_ ; 12. cámera _2_ ; 13. féderal _2_ ; 14. práctically _3_ ; 15. fámily _2_ ; 16. témperature _3_

Practice 2   2. grád uᵂa te; 3. a p p l íʸa n c e; 4. g e ʸó g r a p h y; 5. c oᵂo p e rá t i o n; 6. p r o n u n c i ʸá t i o n; 7. s i t uᵂá t i o n; 8. e x p e r í ʸe n c e; 9. pó ᵂe t r y

Practice 3   3. n éʸo n _2_ ; 4. p e'o p l e _1_ ; 5. s o c í ʸe t y _2_ ; 6. b e l íʸe v e _1_ ; 7. q u í ʸe t _2_ ; 8. s u'i t _1_ ; 9. só c i a l _1_ ; 10. i m m é d i ʸa t e _2_ ; 11. z oᵂó l o g y _2_ ; 12. z o'o _1_

Practice 4   2. búsiness _2_ ; 3. márriage _2_ ; 4. quíetly _3_ ; 5. próblem _2_ ; 6. compáre _2_ ; 7. ínteresting _3_ ; 8. corréction _3_ ; 9. géneral _2_ ; 10. unáble _3_ ; 11. belíeve _2_ ; 12. awákened _3_ ; 13. políce _2_ ; 14. nátional _3_ ; 15. arríve _2_ ; 16. président _3_

Syllable Patterns

′ ‿ ‿	‿ ′ ‿	′ ‿	‿ ′
quietly	December	business	compare
interesting	correction	marriage	believe
national	unable	problem	police
president	awakened	general	arrive

UNIT 6

Practice 1

B: Ĭ thoúght yŏu saĭd kíck ĭt.

A: We'ře nót plaÿing sóccĕr.

B: Weĺl, Í dĭdn't knów thãt.

Practice 5

Jack:	A camping trip?	Sylvia:	mmmmmm (enthusiastic)
Jack:	A fishing trip?	Sylvia:	mmmmmmmm (unenthusiastic)
Jack:	Renting a house on the ocean?	Sylvia:	mmmmmmm (lukewarm)
Jack:	A month in New York City?	Sylvia:	mmmmmmm (lukewarm)
Jack:	A trip to Hawaii?	Sylvia:	mmmmmmmmm (enthusiastic)
Jack:	Two weeks in Paris?	Sylvia:	mmmmmmmm (unenthusiastic)

UNIT 7

Practice 4 1. a; 2. a; 3. b; 4. a; 5. b; 6. b; 7. b; 8. b

Practice 6 [iy] words: 5. bead, 7. police, 11. medium, 14. deep, 15. either; [ɪ] words: 1. live, 3. rhythm, 10. build, 13. been; Not [iy] or [ɪ]: 2. alive, 4. rhyme, 6. bread, 8. ice, 9. guide, 12. medicine, 16. their

UNIT 8

Practice 3 1. b; 2. a; 3. b; 4. a; 5. a; 6. a; 7. a; 8. a

Practice 4 1. c; 2. a; 3. a; 4. b; 5. b; 6. c

Practice 5 pin [ɪ], seller [ɛ], fill [ɪ], hair [ɛ], lit [ɪ], wet [ɛ], edge [ɛ], wait [ey], pen [ɛ], late [ey] (Bingo: Column 2)

Practice 6

Jesse James was the leader of one of the most famous bands of outlaws in the United States. He was born in Missouri in 1847. During the Civil War, he joined a group of Southern raiders who attacked Northern soldiers. When the South was defeated, Jesse and his brother Frank turned to a life of crime.

Jesse and Frank formed a gang of outlaws, and for sixteen years their daring crimes terrorized people in the central states. They robbed banks, stagecoaches, and even trains, but always managed to escape the law. A large reward of $10,000 was offered for Jesse's capture—dead or alive.

In 1881, Jesse decided to settle down in St. Joseph, Missouri. He bought a house, grew a beard, changed his name to Tom Howard, and moved in with his family and two members of his gang, Bob and Charley Ford.

Thinking about the reward money, Bob Ford had been secretly planning to kill Jesse James for months so he could collect the money. Finally, in 1882, he carried out his plan. As Jesse James was standing on a chair in the house, dusting a picture on the wall, Ford pulled out his gun and shot James in the back of the head.

Even though James had murdered innocent people, he was a legend. When people heard about how he had been betrayed by a member of his gang, they mourned his death and cursed the man who murdered him—"that dirty little coward who shot Tom Howard."

Practice 7 2. When [ɛ], heavy [ɛ], rain [ey], came [ey], they [ey], raised [ey], little [ɪ]; 3. Then [ɛ], rain [ey], steadily [ɛ]; 4. Jesse [ɛ], James [ey], famous [ey], West [ɛ], didn't [ɪ]; 5. waited [ey], patiently [ey], message [ɛ], said [ɛ], send [ɛ]; 6. distance [ɪ], speck [ɛ], came [ey]

UNIT 9

Practice 2 1. a; 2. b; 3. b; 4. a; 5. a; 6. a; 7. b; 8. b

UNIT 10

Practice 3 2. different; 3. different; 4. same; 5. different; 6. different; 7. same; 8. same; 9. different; 10. same

UNIT 11

Practice 3 2. one [ə], block [ɑ], from [ə]; 3. tough [ə], job [ɑ]; 4. stopped [ɑ], bus [ə], suddenly [ə]; 5. cup [ə], hot [ɑ], touch [ə]; 6. one [ə], donkey [ɑ], monkeys [ə], hundred [ə], hungry [ə], hogs [ɑ]

Practice 4 1. b; 2. a; 3. b; 4. b; 5. b; 6. a; 7. a; 8. b; 9. b; 10. a

Practice 5 socks, robber, once, buddy, hot, nut, shut, lock, done, color, Don, bucks, body, cup, luck, cut, box, duck, shot (Bingo: Row 3)

UNIT 12

Practice 2 Keller, blunder, lack, blonder, once, lock, color, wants, gust, guest, Don, hum (Bingo: Row 3)

UNIT 13

Practice 5 2. different; 3. different; 4. same; 5. same; 6. same; 7. different; 8. different; 9. same; 10. different; 11. different; 12. different

Practice 6 [ər] words: 1. word, 6. work, 8. her, 9. heard; [or] words: 3. war, 4. born, 10. horn, 11. warm; [ɑr] words: 2. large, 5. hard, 7. heart, 12. guard

Practice 7 Situation 1: Birds of a feather flock together. Situation 2: The early bird gets the worm. Situation 3: A bird in the hand is worth two in the bush.

UNIT 15

Practice 2 1. b; 2. a; 3. b; 4. b; 5. b; 6. a; 7. b; 8. a

Practice 4   2. d; 3. i; 4. a; 5. g; 6. f; 7. h; 8. b; 9. e

Practice 5   1. black and blue; 2. put up with him; 3. a foot in the door; 4. suit yourself

UNIT 16

Practice 3

A Bundle of Phobias

Everyone is afraid of something, and some people are afraid of a lot of things. A phobia is an unreasonable or irrational fear or dislike of something. Some phobias are shared by many people. Many people, for example, are claustrophobic; they feel afraid or panicky in small, crowded places. Other fears, such as the fear of being in a wide open space, are rare. Listen to this dialogue between a therapist and a patient who has more than his share of phobias.

Therapist:	Now, Mr. Swanson, why don't you just lie down and tell me what frightens you.
Mr. Swanson:	It's so hard to know where to begin. For one thing, I'm afraid of heights.
Therapist:	Uh huh. Acrophobia. And what happens when you're in a high place?
Mr. Swanson:	Well, if I look down, my head starts spinning. I feel sick to my stomach.
Therapist:	Well, there's an easy solution to that—just avoid high places. What else? What else frightens you?
Mr. Swanson:	Well, flying. I'm afraid of flying. And spiders. Then there are loud noises, the night, darkness, bright lights.
Therapist:	I see. That's quite a long list of things to be afraid of, Mr. Swanson.
Mr. Swanson:	I wish that were all, doctor. I don't like to be in small, crowded places, or near fire or ice, and I'm also afraid of riding in cars. Can you help me?

UNIT 17

Practice 2   1. no final consonant; 2. final consonant; 3. final consonant; 4. no final consonant; 5. final consonant; 6. final consonant; 7. no final consonant; 8. final consonant; 9. final consonant

Practice 3   1. a; 2. a; 3. a; 4. a; 5. a; 6. a; 7. b; 8. a; 9. a

Practice 5

Although Henry Ford did not invent the automobile, he was the person most responsible for the growth of the automobile industry. Ford was a self-taught mechanic who had two important ideas. First, he wanted to lower the price of automobiles so more Americans could afford them. To do this, he introduced mass production. In 1908 he designed the famous Model T Ford, a strong car that was easy to repair. In his first year of production, he sold 11,000 Model Ts. By 1925, his company produced 9,000 cars a day, at a price of under $300 each.

Ford also had a revolutionary idea about workers and wages. Mass production was efficient, but it made the worker's job boring and tiring. Workers often missed work or quit after a short time, and production decreased. Ford decided to raise his workers' wages from the usual $3 a day to $5 a day. As a result, his workers stayed on the job, and automobile production increased. Ford raised his workers' standard of living and at the same time sold more automobiles.

Ford's success, however, made him stubborn. He did not make major changes in his Model T for nearly twenty years. During that time, other companies like General Motors began to produce better and more stylish cars. Although Ford Motor Company continued to make money, it lost its position as the leading automobile manufacturer and never regained it.

UNIT 18

Practice 1 1b. 3; 2a. 2, b. 3; 3a. 4, b. 5; 4a. 1, b. 2; 5a. 2, b. 3; 6a. 1, b. 2; 7a. 2, b. 3; 8a. 1, b. 2

All of the present verbs in Practice 1 end in a __[t]__ or __[d]__ sound. The past tense ending in these verbs is pronounced as a new _syllable_ .

Practice 2 1b. [pt]; 2a. [l], b. [ld]; 3a. [tʃ], b. [tʃ t]; 4a. [g], b. [gd]; 5a. [sk], b. [skt]; 6a. [v], b. [vd]; 7a. [m], b. [md]; 8a. [yuw], b. [yuwd]

None of the present verbs in Practice 2 ends in [t] or [d]. Therefore, the past tense ending (is / is not) pronounced as an extra syllable.

Practice 7 1. did; 2. do; 3. did; 4. did; 5. do

UNIT 19

Practice 4 1. b; 2. a; 3. a; 4. b; 5. a; 6. a; 7. b; 8. b

UNIT 20

Practice 6 1. b; 2. a; 3. c; 4. b; 5. c; 6. a

UNIT 21

Practice 3 2. [s]; 3. [z]; 4. [z]; 5. [z]; 6. [z]; 7. [s]; 8. [s]; 9. [s]; 10. [z]; 11. [s]; 12. [z]

Practice 4 1. a; 2. a; 3. b; 4. a; 5. b; 6. b; 7. a; 8. a; 9. a; 10. b; 11. a; 12. b

UNIT 22

Practice 3 [s] words: 1. super, 7. promising, 11. exercise, 15. nice; [ʃ] words: 2. sure, 9. expansion, 10. racial, 14. ocean; [z] words: 4. result, 5. visit, 8. easier, 12. museum; [ʒ] words: 3. casual, 6. vision, 13. massage, 16. pleasure

UNIT 23

Practice 2 1. b; 2. b; 3. a; 4. a; 5. a; 6. b; 7. a; 8. b; 9. b

UNIT 24

Practice 2 2. [ks], taxes, yes; 3. [l], smiles, no; 4. [tʃ], sandwiches, yes; 5. [ow], windows, no; 6. [z], prizes, yes; 7. [f], leaves, no; 8. [s], buses, yes; 9. [z], exercises, yes; 10. [r], mothers, no; 11. [t], states, no; 12. [θ], months ([mənts]), no

UNIT 25

Practice 3 1. b; 2. a; 3. b; 4. a; 5. b; 6. a; 7. b; 8. a

UNIT 26

Practice 2 2. yes; 3. no; 4. yes; 5. no; 6. yes; 7. yes; 8. no; 9. no

Practice 3 rim, king, Tim, sung, Bam!, some, singer, ban, kin, Jan, sinner, tin (Bingo: Column 3)

UNIT 27

Practice 4 2. d; 3. g; 4. e; 5. a; 6. h; 7. i; 8. f; 9. c; 10. j

UNIT 28

Practice 3 2. e; 3. g; 4. o; 5. m; 6. f; 7. k; 8. l; 9. d; 10. a; 11. n; 12. b; 13. i; 14. j; 15. h

UNIT 29

Practice 2 1. a; 2. b; 3. b; 4. b; 5. a; 6. a

UNIT 31

Practice 3 1. A: profit, organ, poetry, politics; 2. A: police, define, dishes, mister; 3. A: parent, matter, potato, demand; 4. A: decent, immense, elbow, seldom

UNIT 32

Practice 1 2. édit: éditor, èditórial, èditórialìze; 3. cómmerce: commércial, commèrcializátion, commércially; 4. públic: publícity, públicìze; 5. phótogràph: photógraphy, phòtográphic, photógrapher; 6. prófit: pròfitéer, prófitable, pròfitabílity; 7. moúntain: moúntainous, moùntaineér; 8. objéctive: objéctify, òbjectívity; 9. mínor: minórity; 10. pérson: persónify, persònificátion; 11. círculàte: círculatòry, cìrculátion; 12. fínànce: fináncial, fìnancíer

Practice 2 1. Cìrculátion, Círculàte, círculatòry; 2. Móuntainous, moùntaineér; 3. Édit, Èditórials, éditor; 4. compéting, còmpetítion, compétitive

Practice 3 1b. duplicate [ət], duplicate [eyt]; 2. associate [ət], associate [eyt]; 3. graduate [eyt], graduate [ət]; 4. estimate [eyt], estimate [ət]

UNIT 33

Practice 3   2a. récord, b. recórd; 3a. rébel, b. rebél; 4a. súspèct, b. suspéct; 5a. cónvìct, b. convíct; 6a. cóndùct, b. condúct; 7a. présent, b. presént; 8a. óbjèct, b. objéct; 9a. cóntràct, b. contráct; 10a. prótèst, b. protést

Practice 4   1. verb; 2. verb; 3. noun; 4. verb; 5. noun; 6. noun; 7. verb

UNIT 34

Practice 1   The rhythm pattern of all four lines is the same.

Practice 4   1. Russia; 2. Alaska; 3. the Nile; 4. the whale; 5. the elephant; 6. California; 7. the Mississippi; 8. Brazil; 9. China; 10. Mount McKinley

UNIT 35

Practice 4   1. or; 2. and; 3. or; 4. or; 5. and; 6. and

Practice 5   1. can't; 2. can't; 3. can; 4. can't; 5. can; 6. can

UNIT 36

Practice 2   2. j; 3. i; 4. a; 5. e; 6. f; 7. h; 8. g; 9. c; 10. d

UNIT 37

Practice 2   2. h; 3. g; 4. i; 5. e; 6. a; 7. j; 8. f; 9. b; 10. d

UNIT 40

Practice 1

A: You're not going to marry that horrible man, are you?

B: I told you to stay out of my life, didn't I?

A: I've always supported your decisions before, haven't I?

B: You're in love with him yourself, aren't you?

A: Your parents don't know about him, do they?

B: You won't tell them, will you?

A: You're afraid they won't like him, aren't you?

B: I don't know what to do. Do you?

 APPENDIX

GROUP A: GAME QUESTIONS AND HINTS

UNIT 6

Practice 4. The Highlighting Game

1. The ge——hisssssssss will be in Los Angeles.   (general)
2. He'll be there next S——hisssssss.   (Sunday)
3. Meet him at T——hisssssss Restaurant.   (Tom's)
4. He'll give you some p——hisssssssss.   (papers)
5. You give him your gu——hisssssssssss.   (gun)

Now Spy B will give you five pieces of information. Each time Spy B speaks, the steam pipe hisses and you don't hear B clearly. You think B said the following, but you must check by asking.

1. Charley? 2. bomb? 3. Dayton? 4. laundry? 5. six?

UNIT 9

Practice 3. Sense or Nonsense?

The _____ _____ when the _____
         E   G   B

hit it with a _____ _____ .
              D   C

UNIT 10

Practice 6. Sense or Nonsense?

_____ last _____ , the _____
     A   B   G   C

pointed his/her _____ at me and shouted, "Give me your
                 D

_____ or your life!" I said, "Okay, okay! Don't _____ me! It's
    I   E

over there—in my _____ ."
                 F

UNIT 18

Practice 4. The Past Tense Game

    1. listen; 2. love; 3. expect; 4. need; 5. play; 6. drop; 7. answer; 8. fix; 9. seem;
10. arrest

UNIT 19

Practice 5. The "th" Game

    1. What's an unlucky number?
    2. What's 10 × 3?
    3. What's the opposite of *unhealthy*?
    4. How do you pronounce T-H-O-R-O-U-G-H?
    5. If you're in the state of Nebraska and you want to go to Kansas, do you go north or south?
    6. What's the opposite of *fat*?
    7. How much is 4,270 × 72?
    8. On your hand you have four fingers and one _____.
    9. What should you say when someone does something nice for you?
    10. Is Los Angeles north or south of San Francisco?
    11. Your parents include your _____ and your _____.

Answers: 1. thirteen; 2. thirty; 3. healthy; 4. [θə́row]; 5. north; 6. thin; 7. about three hundred thousand (exactly 307,440); 8. thumb; 9. thank you (or thanks); 10. south; 11. mother, father

UNIT 20

Practice 10. The [p, b, f, v, w] Game

    1. What is the name of the sixth letter of the alphabet?
    2. What is the general name for foods like apples, pears, cherries, and strawberries?
    3. What's the opposite of *sad*?
    4. What's the name of the sport where tall people throw balls through a hoop?
    5. Some people speak Spanish; some people speak English; some people speak Korean. Spanish, English, and Korean are _____.
    6. What's the opposite of *hate*?
    7. What's 50 + 5?
    8. What color do you get when you mix red and white together?
    9. What's the opposite of *enemy*?
    10. What's the superlative of *good*?
    11. What number comes after ten?
    12. What's the opposite of *small*?

Answers: 1. F [ɛf]; 2. fruit; 3. happy; 4. basketball; 5. languages; 6. love; 7. fifty-five; 8. pink; 9. friend; 10. best; 11. eleven; 12. big

UNIT 37

Practice 4. Speaking
Student A's Picture

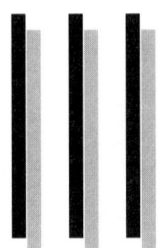
UNIT 6

Practice 4. The Highlighting Game

       1. judge? 2. Saturday? 3. Tim's? 4. paintings? 5. gum?

       Now give Spy A this information.

       1. The chief wants you to call Ch——hissssssssssssss.   (Chester)
       2. Chester has a b——hisssssssssssss for you.   (bag)
       3. Take the bag to the Da——hissssssss Hotel at exactly 6:55.   (Davis)
       4. Leave it in the l——hisssssssssssss.   (lobby)
       5. Leave the hotel before s——hissssssss o'clock.   (seven)

UNIT 9

Practice 3. Sense or Nonsense?

The _____ wearing the _____ _____
          F   D   B

was _____ and _____ .
          A   A

UNIT 10

Practice 6. Sense or Nonsense?

The _____ _____ was _____ so he/she went to
          G   C   G

his/her _____ and asked for some _____ . "I know you don't
             C   I

have _____ ," he/she said, "but if you _____ me, you'll give
          H   E

me yours. Next _____ I'll pay you back, even if I have to sell my
               B

_____ ."
   F

UNIT 18

Practice 4. The Past Tense Game

1. open; 2. walk (The *l* is silent: *wal̸k.*); 3. help; 4. suggest; 5. count; 6. move; 7. change; 8. like; 9. practice; 10. die

UNIT 19

Practice 5. The "th" Game

1. Is New York City north or south of Boston?
2. What do you call the top part of the leg, above the knee?
3. The word *dead* is an adjective. What is the noun?
4. How much is 1,000 × 3?
5. What's the name of the day after Wednesday?
6. If you're in California and you want to go to Washington State, do you go north or south?
7. How much is 850 × 36?
8. What is the plural of the word *this*?
9. How do you pronounce T-H-O-U-G-H?
10. Where can you see a movie or a play?
11. Your mother's son is your _____ .

Answers: 1. south; 2. the thigh; 3. death; 4. 3,000; 5. Thursday; 6. north; 7. about 30,000 (exactly 30,600); 8. these; 9. [ðow]; 10. in a theater; 11. brother

UNIT 20

Practice 10. The [p, b, f, v, w] Game

1. What's a common plural word used to refer to human beings?
2. What's 5 × 5?
3. You kiss with your _____ .
4. What do people do in elections?
5. What's a word that means "not ever"?
6. Two common spices are salt and _____ .
7. These animals live in water.
8. What's a synonym for *start*?
9. What's the opposite of *rude*?
10. What do the words *windy, rainy, sunny,* and *cloudy* describe?
11. These sea animals are the largest animals on earth.
12. You have these on your hands.

Answers: 1. people; 2. twenty-five; 3. lips; 4. vote; 5. never; 6. pepper; 7. fish (or whales, dolphins, squid, octopi); 8. begin; 9. polite; 10. weather; 11. whales; 12. fingers

Practice 4. Speaking
Student B's Picture

GLOSSARY

AFFRICATE CONSONANTS: Consonants that combine a stop and fricative. [tʃ] and [dʒ] are affricate consonants. (Unit 4, p. 11)

ASPIRATION: A puff of air pronounced with the beginning stop consonants [p, t, k]. (Unit 4, p. 11)

COMPOUND NOUNS: Two nouns used together as one noun, such as *railroad*. Compound nouns have a special stress-pitch pattern. (Unit 33, p. 115)

CONTENT WORDS: Nouns, verbs, adjectives, and adverbs. Content words are usually pronounced more strongly than function words. (Unit 6, p. 16)

CLUSTER, CONSONANT CLUSTER: Two or more consonants together, for example *spring*. (Unit 29, p. 100)

DIPHTHONG: A vowel plus [w] or [y]. [aw], [ay], and [oy] are diphthongs. (Unit 3, p. 7)

FRICATIVE CONSONANTS: Consonants that are produced by obstructing but not completely blocking the air flow. Fricatives have a noisy sound. The fricatives are [f, v, θ , ð, s, z, ʃ, ʒ, h]. (Unit 4, p. 10)

FUNCTION WORDS: Articles, short prepositions, conjunctions, auxiliary verbs, pronouns. Function words are usually pronounced less strongly than content words. (Unit 6, p. 16)

HIGHLIGHTING: Use of strong stress and high (or very low) pitch to show a word is important. (Unit 6, p. 18)

IMPURE VOWELS: Vowels that end in a short [y] or [w] sound. [iy], [ey], [uw], [ow] are impure vowels. (Unit 3, p. 8)

INTONATION: The melody of speech; the patterning of high and low notes. (Unit 6, p. 19)

JOINING: Pronouncing words together smoothly, without breaks. (Unit 6, p. 18)

LAX VOWELS: Vowels pronounced toward the center of the mouth, with relaxed muscles. [ɪ], [ɛ] and [ʊ] are examples of lax vowels. (Unit 3, p. 7)

NASAL CONSONANTS: Consonants that are pronounced when air passes out through the nose. [m], [n], [ŋ] are nasal consonants. (Unit 26, p. 90)

PHONETIC SYMBOLS, PHONETIC ALPHABET: Symbols such as [æ] and [ə] that are used to represent sounds. (Unit 1, p. 2)

PITCH: The musical note on which a word or syllable is pronounced. (Unit 5, p. 13)

REDUCED VOWELS: Unstressed vowels pronounced with an [ə] or [ɪ] sound. (Unit 31, p. 107)

REDUCED WORDS: Unstressed words with reduced vowels or dropped consonants; usually "grammar" or function words like prepositions or articles. (Unit 6, p. 17)

SCHWA: The vowel sound [ə] as in the word *cup*. In many words, unstressed vowels are reduced to a short [ə] sound. (Unit 10, p. 35)

STOP CONSONANTS: Consonants that are produced by a brief, complete stoppage of the air flow. [p, b, t, d, k, g] are stop consonants. (Unit 4, p. 10)

STRESS: Stressed vowels are long and loud. They are often pronounced with high pitch. In a word that has both primary and secondary stress, the vowel with primary stress is pronounced more strongly than the vowel with the secondary stress. (Unit 5, p. 13, Unit 32, p. 112)

STRONG SYLLABLES: Syllables that have stressed vowels. (Unit 6, p. 16)

SYLLABLE: A beat of a word consisting of a vowel and one or more consonants. The word, *visit*, for example, has two syllables. (Unit 5, p. 13)

TENSE VOWELS: Vowels pronounced with tension in the muscles of the mouth, especially the vowels [iy], [ey], [uw], and [ow], which are pronounced with the lips spread or rounded. (Unit 3, p. 7)

THOUGHT GROUPS: Meaningful groups of words or phrases pronounced together. (Unit 6, p. 18)

UNRELEASED CONSONANTS: Final consonants that are pronounced and held, but not strongly released. (Unit 17, p. 61)

VOCAL ORGANS: Parts of the mouth, tongue, and throat used to produce sounds. (Unit 4, p. 9)

VOICED SOUNDS: Sounds produced when the vocal cords vibrate. [b], [z], and [dʒ] are examples of voiced sounds. (Unit 4, p. 10)

VOICELESS SOUNDS: Sounds produced without vocal cord vibration. [p], [s], and [tʃ] are examples or voiceless sounds. (Unit 4, p. 10)

WEAK SYLLABLES: Syllables that have unstressed vowels. (Unit 6, p. 16)